BISON
BOOKS

W9-BAL-572

Erastus F. Beadle

# Ham, Eggs, and Corn Cake

A Nebraska Territory Diary

Erastus F. Beadle

Introduction by Ronald C. Naugle

University of Nebraska Press

Lincoln and London

⊗

Library of Congress Cataloging-in-
Publication Data
Beadle, Erastus Flavel, 1821–1894
[To Nebraska in '57]
Ham, eggs, and corn cake : a Nebraska
Territory diary / Erastus F. Beadle ; in-
troduction by Ronald C. Naugle.
p. cm.
Originally published as: To Nebraska
in '57 : a diary of Erastus F. Beadle.
New York: New York Public Library, 1923.
ISBN 0-8032-6187-x (pbk. : alk. paper)
1. Beadle, Erastus Flavel, 1821–1894—
Diaries.   2. Pioneers—Nebraska—Diaries.
3. Frontier and pioneer life—Nebraska.
4. Nebraska—Social life and customs—
19th century.   5. Omaha Region (Neb.)—
Social life and customs—19th century.
6. Omaha Region (Neb.)—Biography.
7. Beadle, Erastus Flavel, 1821–1894—
Journeys—Middle West.   8. Frontier
and pioneer life—Middle West.
I. Title.
F666.B36 2001
978.2'02'092—dc21
2001027704

# Contents

# Maps and Illustrations

RONALD C. NAUGLE

# Introduction

The lure of the West is an indelible part of American history, legend, and folklore. The cast of characters and human drama associated with the development of the United States and its expansion westward to fill the continent have shaped American character and values. They have defined what America is; sadly, for others they have illustrated what America is not. The myth and the reality at times appear inseparable. What is truth? What is fiction?

The diary of Erastus Flavel Beadle is the diary of a man lured by the myth of the West as a place of adventure, a new start, a chance to get rich. It is also the diary of a man who faced realities that drew him back to the East, from which he had come. The diary is one man's brief account of life in Nebraska Territory in 1857, and it provides snapshots of a human drama as it plays out in business, culture, and politics. Beadle's diary furnishes a picture of the reality of one small piece of the nineteenth-century American West and a glimpse into the dreams and hopes of a group of men for the creation and future of Saratoga, a western city to rival all others (see map 1).

Erastus F. Beadle was born in Pierstown, New York, (immediately north of Cooperstown) on 11 September 1821, the son of Flavel and Polly Fuller Beadle.[1] There is little recorded information about his early life. Biographical dictionaries and encyclopedias contain brief and sometimes conflicting information, but there is general agreement that during Beadle's early years his parents moved several times, once as far west as Kalamazoo County, Michigan, in hope of finding success in farming.

In 1835, during a brief stay near Fredonia, New York, where his parents did odd jobs for farmers, young Erastus obtained employment as a farm hand. He remained there after his parents moved back to the Cooperstown area; consequently, at age fourteen he was on his own. During his approximately six months in Fredonia, Beadle became acquainted with the local printer and soon learned the basics of the printing trade, a path that would eventually lead to his fame and fortune.[2]

After his lone stay in Fredonia, Beadle moved to Cooperstown, where he became an apprentice at the printing house of H. and E. Phinney. He stayed many years with this firm, following it to new offices in Buffalo, New York, after the Cooperstown printing house burned in 1847. Just the year before he had married Mary Ann Pennington.[3]

Beadle's printing and publishing career flourished with the move to Buffalo. Within a short time he took a new position as a stereotyper for the *Buffalo Commercial Advertiser*, and three years later, in 1850, he went into business with his brother, Irwin, establishing a stereotype foundry. During this time he also decided to try his hand at publishing and, in 1852, launched his first magazine, *The Youth's Casket: An Illustrated Magazine for the Young*.

With the success of *The Youth's Casket*, Erastus and Irwin sold the foundry and established their own publishing company. By 1856 they were publishing a second magazine, *The Home: A Fireside Companion and Guide for the Wife, the Mother, the Sister and the Daughter*. The name was later changed to *Beadles Home Monthly*. In 1856 Robert Adams became a partner in the firm; this is the Robert to whom Beadle frequently refers in his journal.[4]

By late summer 1856 Erastus Beadle was thirty-four years of age, had been married for ten years, and had three children: Irwin Flavel, age nine; Sophia, age seven; and Walter Hamilton, age six.[5] The fondness with which Beadle refers to his wife in his journal as "Mate" and his frequent expressions of missing her and the children, whom he hopes will join him soon, suggest it was a happy marriage.

Over the course of the preceding twenty years he had established both a family and himself, first as a printer and subsequently as a publisher. In partnership with his brother and Adams, he controlled a publishing house that was producing two popular magazines.

The publishing career of Erastus Beadle thereafter is well-documented. So too is the House of Beadle and Adams, which developed from the partnership with Robert Adams.[6] The Buffalo firm relocated to New York City in 1858 and by 1860 was publishing a series of adventure novels, which sold for ten cents each. The dime novels were such a success and in such high demand that they revolutionized the publishing industry and reshaped the reading habits of millions of Americans.

While Beadle could not have known his future and how prominently he would figure in the publishing industry, he must certainly have viewed his prospects in August of 1856 with some optimism. Yet it was at this very point in his life that a fascination with the West lured him to visit Omaha, Nebraska Territory, and led to his decisions to leave the publishing house in the hands of his brother and partner, return to Omaha the following spring—with the intent of making his fortune in real estate—and eventually resettle there with his family.

In August 1856 Omaha City, Nebraska Territory, was a place of great promise. So too were more than a dozen other burgeoning communities along the eastern edge of the territory, where promoters and investors had placed their faith. Indeed the First Territorial Legislature in 1855 incorporated fourteen town sites that used the word "city" in their names and which their developers promoted as a new Chicago, New York, or Philadelphia.[7]

The territory was just two years old when Beadle made his first trip out; its population was booming. From 30 May 1854, when President Franklin Pierce signed the Kansas-Nebraska Act, officially opening the region to settlement, the territory had expanded from a few squatters living in cabins along the western side of the Missouri River to a population of 2,732 just six months later. The population nearly doubled the following year to 4,494 and more than redoubled by 1856 to 10,716. In 1857 the territory's population was estimated at nearly twenty thousand.[8]

Land prices in 1857 also reflected optimism. Riverfront lots in some towns sold for as much as ten thousand dollars; those three or four blocks back brought two thousand dollars; even those as much as half a mile away brought twelve hundred dollars.[9] In most cases the sellers had acquired these properties either by preemption or for just a few dollars only two to three years earlier.

The real estate frenzy up and down the Missouri River was fueled by the hope of each group of promoters that their city would become the gateway city of the transcontinental railroad; indeed, the very legislation that created the Nebraska territory was driven by the desire to make possible the Platte River Valley route for the great railroad to the west, a route that over the preceding twelve years had proven itself by overland immigrant travel to Utah, California, and Oregon.

A vast area once perceived as the Great American Desert, worthless to white people for agricultural development, and which just twenty years earlier Congress had designated permanent Indian country, was now valuable. For promoters from Iowa, Chicago, and points further east, who had interests tied to the Platte Valley route, the concept of a permanent Indian frontier had to give way to territorial organization and settlement.

Few of the towns would live up to their promoters' hopes, and Omaha would soon maneuver itself into political and commercial dominance, but in 1856 the mood everywhere was one of great optimism. Governor Mark W. Izard, in addressing the Territorial Legislature in January 1857, praised the continuing optimism in Nebraska's future and pointed to the churches, schools, and commercial buildings under construction as evidence of the prosperity in Nebraska's towns and cities.[10]

Beadle's diary is the record of his journey to Omaha in 1857 and covers the time from 9 March to 1 October 1857. He does not explain why he had decided to visit Omaha the preceding August; he makes only slight references to his having been there the previous fall. On 19 August 1857, he notes in his diary the anniversary of his having left Buffalo for Omaha. No indication of how long he stayed nor the precise business arrangement he negotiated is included. Apparently, he returned home from the first visit to put his affairs in order and make preparations for returning to Omaha in the spring to establish himself and prepare a home for his family to join him later.

The venture that drew Beadle back to Omaha in 1857 was the development of a town that was to be called Saratoga, located between Omaha and Florence. Saratoga's unique feature was a sulphur springs near the Missouri River, around which its developers planned to build a grand hotel called the Trinity House.[11] They also hoped to attract other entrepreneurs who would establish businesses that would make the town commercially viable as well as attractive to tourists.

The company was named the Sulphur Springs Land Company, and to attract residents who would build homes in this new city, the company offered, in Beadle's words, "256 lots to churches, schools and individuals who will build before July first [1857]."[12] Beadle's duties with the company were to supervise the drawing of lots for the shareholders (who were entitled to fifteen lots each), promote the town, and give away the free lots to people who would build on them. Beadle was to receive a free lot and an undisclosed amount of money as compensation for his services to the company.

Several of Beadle's new business associates had a New York connection, which might in part explain his interest in the Sulphur Springs and Saratoga venture. Taylor G. Goodwill, chairman of the executive committee of the Sulphur Springs Land Company, and upon whose death Beadle succeeded in that capacity, was from upstate New York.[13] Goodwill owned the actual sulphur springs and probably named the town Saratoga after a popular mineral springs resort at Saratoga, New York.

LeRoy Tuttle, treasurer of the company, was also from New York. Tuttle had at one time been a banker in Cooperstown but later had moved to Ilion, New York. In 1855 he came to Omaha to be cashier of the Western Exchange Fire and Marine Insurance Company, which was also licensed to do general banking.[14]

Two days after his arrival in Omaha Beadle called on John H. Kellum, having made an acquaintance with him the previous fall. Although not directly connected with the Saratoga project, Kellum was from Washington County, New York, and had come to Omaha in 1856 to open a bank with backing from Frank D. Gridley, a Buffalo banker with whom Beadle had done business and whom he considered a friend.[15] Gridley arrived in Saratoga on 21 May to visit Kellum and inspect the bank.

On 9 March 1857, Beadle began his journey, which would take him twenty-one days. While his second trip out to Nebraska was less direct than his return to Buffalo had been the previous August, and was made up to nine days longer by stops to visit friends, relatives, and business acquaintances on the way, his diary provides a fascinating, detailed account of the difficulties of travel in the mid-nineteenth century. The connections that had to be made between such various conveyances as ferries, steamers, rail cars, and coaches and the hazards associated with each suggest a seriousness of purpose that must have accompanied the decision to travel any great distance. Beadle faced most of the mishaps of his trip with resolve, including the breakdown of his coach, which forced him to walk the last six miles of his journey.

Beadle's interest was in the development of the town of Saratoga, not Omaha, but he had to live in Omaha and, for a period of time, use Omaha as his base of operation. During the first few days, he reconnected with businessmen he had met the previous fall, principally a Mr. Cook and a Mr. Warner. While the living accommodations in Omaha in Beadle's view were rather primitive, Mr. Warner arranged for Beadle to board where he did, in the household of Experience Estabrook, U.S. attorney for the territory.[16] As a result Beadle's Omaha accommodations were far better than most.

There were few laws governing the development of towns when Nebraska became a territory in 1854. The Pre-Emption Law of 1841 allowed individual citizens to preempt 160 acres of public-domain land and file a claim to it after marking the corners and living on it for five days and nights. The federal townsites Act of 1844 allowed towns, or an organized company of town developers, the same preemption rights on 320 acres. Legal title to land, however, could not be obtained until the land was surveyed. Groups of enterprising individuals, such as those with whom Beadle had associated, could organize a company, elect officers, claim 320 acres, and also, as individuals, claim 160 acres each, all adjacent to each other.

Taylor Goodwill had purchased a claim of 160 acres that included the sulphur springs from a William Clancy in 1854. Goodwill wanted to build the resort hotel at the springs and develop the town to rival all others in the territory. One hundred and sixty acres was not enough for such a grand venture, so Goodwill and a group of other like-minded promoters incorporated the Sulphur Springs Land Company in October 1856 to claim 320 acres in the name of Saratoga and begin the acquisition of individual quarter sections to acquire land for the city. They eventually acquired a total of twenty-three hundred acres.[17]

*The Nebraskian*, a territorial newspaper established to promote Omaha, announced on 22 October 1856 the incorporation of the Sulphur Springs Land Company, whose purpose was to develop a town called Saratoga. The officers and board of directors were duly noted. The president was Thomas Hart Benton Jr., son of Missouri's expansionist senator, who had strongly supported the formation of Nebraska Territory. Other officers were LeRoy Tuttle, treasurer, and William Young Brown, secretary. Members of the executive committee were Taylor Goodwill, A. F. Salisbury, and Edwin Patton; the remaining board members were Addison Cochran, James C. Mitchell, C. B. Smith, and Samuel M. Owens.[18] The location of Saratoga today would lie between Fort Street on the north and Locust Street on the south, and between 36th Street on the west and Carter Lake on the east (see map 2).[19]

To protect presurvey claims, such as those only cornerstaked by the Sulphur Springs Land Company, it was common practice to organize a claim club. These were groups of claimants who organized to establish a set of laws for governing themselves and protecting their claims, by force if necessary, against claim jumpers. Claim clubs initially operated outside the law or in the absence of law, but the first session of the Nebraska Territorial Legislature gave them a measure of credibility by recognizing and defining their activities through law. For purposes of protecting the group's claims, claim clubs could appoint a subcommittee of enforcers and a leader, who was often referred to as the sheriff. A would-be claimant who ignored the system and tried to stake land already claimed by one of the club's members would be visited by the sheriff and enforcers and threatened or tortured until he relinquished or denounced his rights to his claim.[20]

Beadle witnessed the effectiveness of this form of justice when the Saratoga Claim Club dealt with a claim jumper who was particularly stubborn about withdrawing his filing. In this case the captain and the regulators, as the sheriff and enforcers were designated, tied a rope around the perpetrator and threw him into the Missouri River three times before he saw the error of his ways.

In his diary Beadle is enthusiastic about the prospects for Saratoga. He comments frequently about the superiority of the site over that of Omaha. He is encouraged by the steady stream of people arriving throughout the late spring and early summer and provides a daily accounting of the steamers arriving at Omaha. When the first steamer, *Florence*, lands at Saratoga on 19 April he is convinced it is the beginning of commercial business for Saratoga. Shortly thereafter he decides to build a warehouse and start his own business.

Beadle's activities in promoting the town probably account for his election as chair of the executive committee on 21 May to replace Taylor Goodwill, who had died of typhoid. Not clear is whether he purchased shares in the company or whether the company's indebtedness to him made him a member of the board. Later diary entries suggest the latter.

Boarding in the home of U.S. Attorney Estabrook put Beadle in a position to meet many prominent persons in Omaha and the territory, such as Governor Izard and Brig. Gen. John M. Thayer, and to witness first hand discussion of territorial political issues he may otherwise have missed. On 10 July he returns home to find Judge Fenner Ferguson and his wife from Bellevue visiting Estabrook. Ferguson was a Democratic candidate for territorial delegate to Congress in the upcoming congressional election, scheduled for 1 August. The discussion centers around a letter Estabrook had received from Nebraska City indicating that Otoe County had pledged its support for Benjamin P. Rankin, also a Democrat, for the same office.

Party affiliation played less of a role in early Nebraska territorial politics than it would later; the Republican Party would not be officially organized for another two years. The Whigs, who would become part of the Republican Party, were declining in number. Most men of ambition in the new territory were Democrats because Franklin Pierce was president when Nebraska Territory was established and had appointed early territorial officers from his own party.

Political campaigns were often heated affairs, replete with personal attacks. Sectional interests were also more important than party affiliation, with the territory frequently dividing at the Platte River. Omaha's dominance in the new territory and its claim to the territorial capitol had rankled many would-be competitors, such as Bellevue, Nebraska City, and Brownville. During the Fourth Territorial Legislature, for example, arguments between the South Platters and North Platters became so heated that guns were drawn, and a rump session reconvened at Florence to talk about J. Sterling Morton's suggestion that the counties south of the Platte seek annexation to Kansas.[21] The issue would emerge with greater seriousness in 1859, when secession conventions were held in Brownsville and Nebraska City and formal petitions were made, only to be rejected by Kansas.

There were often numerous candidates for few offices, and most had political experience. Judge Ferguson was one of three federal judges appointed to the territory in 1854.[22] Rankin had been the first territorial treasurer and since March of 1856 had been U.S. marshal for the territory. He would run again for Congress in 1859 and lose to Estabrook.[23] Bird B. Chapman, who came to Omaha in 1854 to establish *The Nebraskian*, to promote the interests of Omaha and later Saratoga, was also a candidate for Congress in 1857.[24] So too was Thayer, brigadier general of the militia, who was running as an Independent. In the end, Ferguson carried the election, but only by a plurality.[25]

Beadle also comments frequently about the condition of the Indians and the number that were camped in the vicinity. He is particularly disturbed by the condition of the Pawnee and their apparent filth and starvation. What Beadle was witnessing was the result of white expansion westward and territorial organization that had mandated the cession of Indian lands. Except for a small parcel for the Omahas eighty-some miles up the Missouri River from Omaha City and an even smaller one for the Pawnee about one hundred miles west on the Loup River, the Indians by 1857 had lost all of their land in the eastern two-thirds of present-day Nebraska.

Because of decades of interaction with fur traders along the Missouri River, the Omaha had experienced a greater degree of western accultura-tion than the Pawnee. The Pawnee whom Beadle saw were the survivors of a once powerful tribe that had dominated central Nebraska. The few who remained near the eastern towns and cities were reduced to total dependency and begging or thievery for survival. It is little wonder that some would resort to stealing an occasional cow from isolated settlers. These incidents regularly set off alarms, accompanied by calls for wiping out the remaining Indians. Fortunately Governor Izard was cautious in responding to these situations to which Beadle refers in his diary.

Beadle's encounter with a Pawnee man named Corax caused him to see the Indian situation in a different light from most of the settlers' views. His host, Estabrook, was obviously a man who possessed a greater degree of sensitivity to the Indians than many whites, and this too influenced Beadle, who later in his diary expressed his disturbance about the wrongs done to the Indians.

While Beadle came to Nebraska to make money, he came with the desire to settle and make a new life for himself and his family. He commented frequently in his diary about missing his family and his expectation that they would soon join him. It was this latter desire that came to the fore toward the end of June when he met a young land speculator, Dick Darling.

Dick Darling, if indeed that was his correct name, was the epitome of a land speculator and gambler. He had staked numerous claims during the previous three years and then sold them when he could make a profit. Because he was still under twenty-one years of age, he could not legally preempt land in his own right. On 26 June Darling took Beadle to see a piece of land some six miles west of Omaha, on which he had staked a claim, and Beadle immediately became excited about the prospects of acquiring it as a place where he and his family could settle.

After seeing Darling's claim Beadle's interests in Saratoga declined. Though chair of the executive committee, his description of his work for Saratoga seems less exciting and more perfunctory. He was offered the job of postmaster for Saratoga and declined. On 20 July, he turned in his bill for services and his resignation.

When Darling finally agreed to trade his claim west of Omaha for Beadle's lots in Saratoga, Beadle immediately made plans to build a shelter on the site and live there the requisite five days in order to file the preemption papers on it. Beadle called his claim Rock Brook Farm, a 240-acre plot just northeast of present-day Rockbrook Shopping Center and west of the juncture of Big Papillion and Rockbrook Creek (Beadle's Nin-na-bah), north of West Center Road (see map 3).

After five days at Rock Brook Farm Beadle returned to Omaha, filed his claim with the Land Office, and began making preparations to return to New York. Why Beadle lost interest in the Saratoga project is not clear. Detectable is that his relationship to LeRoy Tuttle had, from the beginning, appeared strained. Diary entries indicate a frustration that Tuttle was not in Omaha when Beadle arrived. On 5 June Beadle comments, "he [Tuttle] talks large for me, and if one half he tells me turns out right I shall be satisfyed [sic]," suggesting that Tuttle exaggerated more than a little.

Perhaps as chairman of the executive committee of the Sulphur Springs Land Company, Beadle had become uneasy with the company's finances. His diary entries reflect his concern over lack of capital and frustration over not knowing whether he would ever be paid for his services to the company.

There were also hints of the coming depression. Diary entries refer to disturbing news from home. Gridley brings him "surprising" news about the closing of a Buffalo business. Other rumblings of economic collapse continue throughout the late summer. When he reaches Chicago on 31 August he hears that the Reciprocity Bank of Buffalo has failed—the bank that had issued all the money he had to travel home.

Within the month Nebraska felt the full brunt of the panic, which resulted in the collapse of most of the territorial financial institutions. The panic was made worse in eastern Nebraska because of the lack of hard money and the desire to promote prosperity.

To increase the amount of money in circulation, the First Territorial Legislature had created banks of issue, allowing them to print money on the name of the bank, often with very little real or sound capital to back up the paper. Known as "wildcat" banks because of the unsoundness of this practice, the banks' money also became known as "wildcat" currency, worth nothing outside the territory and nothing at all if the bank collapsed.

The first Territorial Legislature, under pressure from Omaha promoters, many of whom were also members of the legislature, chartered two such banks, one of which was the Western Exchange Fire and Marine Insurance Company, to do business as the Western Exchange Bank. The bank's primary investors were the same as those of the Sulphur Springs Land Company.

The Second Territorial Legislature chartered five more banks, among them Fontenelle Bank, owned by Thomas Hart Benton Jr., and the Bank of Florence, owned by James C. Mitchell, both of whom were directors of the Sulphur Springs Land Company.[26] During the third Territorial Legislature's session, six more bank bills were passed, but Governor Izard vetoed all six. Two bills, however, were passed over his veto, creating the Bank of DeSoto and Bank of Tekamah, both owned by William Young Brown, secretrary of the Sulphur Springs Land Company.[27]

The same legislature repealed a law that had been passed by the second legislature making it a crime to open a bank without legislative charter. This opened a floodgate of banking activity and made it easier for Beadle's friend and Buffalo banker Frank Gridley to open a branch of his bank in Saratoga and at the same time become a major investor in the Western Exchange.

The collusion of interest, lack of real capital, and few assets created a situation ripe for disaster. The bust came on 23 September 1857, when the Western Exchange collapsed, leaving individuals with more than one hundred fifty thousand dollars in losses. The collapse of the Bank of Tekamah followed, leaving personal losses of ninety thousand dollars.[28]

Saratoga was bust; so too were the dreams of many for the city's future. There had been talk of the great resort and grand hotel around the sulphur springs; others had formed a board to begin plans for creating a University of Nebraska at Saratoga, undoubtedly to enhance the desire to invest in the community. Instead, by October 1857 Saratoga was deserted. Omaha had lost three quarters of its population.[29]

Beadle left Omaha with virtually nothing, but he was luckier than most. He still had his claim to Rock Brook Farm, which he would later sell. He was reunited with his family, which had moved back to

Cooperstown, and he reentered the publishing venture with his brother, Irwin, and Robert Adams.

While Beadle's publishing career has been carefully documented by Albert Johannsen in his two-volume work, *The House of Beadle and Adams*, little is known about Beadle's personal life after his Nebraska experience. He continued to keep a diary throughout the remainder of his life, but his daughter, Sophie, destroyed the volumes upon his death.[30]

Beadle published 5,258 novels in 718 series, 313 handbooks and guides, and 718 periodical issues.[31] *The Youth's Casket* ceased publication in 1857. In 1858 the three partners moved the publishing house to New York City. From 1858 to 1860 Irwin established his own business, a bookstore and publishing house, and published a variety of ten-cent handbooks and songbooks, while Beadle and Adams continued publication of *The Home*. In 1859 they began publishing a series of handbooks and guides for families and youth. They also published a series of songbooks and a series entitled *Speakers*, which ran until 1886. Yet another series called *Dialogues* ran until 1894.

In May 1860 Irwin rejoined his brother and Adams, and the following month the firm launched the Dime Novel series with the publication on 9 June of *Malaeska, The Indian Wife of the White Hunter* by Mrs. Ann S. Stephens. The Dime Novel series, which focused on the adventures, hardships, and struggles of American pioneers carving a civilization out of the wilderness, was actually Irwin's idea, but it was enthusiastically embraced by Beadle, in part perhaps because of his Nebraska Territory experience.

The Dime Novel format was only one of more than fifty different publication formats produced by the publishing house of Beadle and Adams, but it is the one for which Beadle is best remembered. It comprised 321 novels, including *Seth Jones; or, The Captives of the Frontier* (1860); *Bill Biddon, Trapper; or, Life in the North-west* (1860); *The Land Claim. A Tale of the Upper Missouri* (1862); *Myrtle, the Child of the Prairie* (1863); *Quindaro; or, The Heroine of Ft. Laramie. A Tale of the Far West* (1865); *Dusky Dick; or, Old Toby Castor's Great Campaign. A Story of the Last Sioux Outbreak* (1872); and *Dick Darling, the Pony Expressman. A Tale of the Old Salt Lake Trail* (1874). The latter title may well have been inspired by Beadle's association with the Dick Darling of his Omaha days. Other formats also continued the western pioneer and adventure themes. Beginning in 1874 the Dime Novel series was succeeded by the New Dime Novel series, most of which were reprints from the first series.

The western motif had attracted a loyal readership by the 1870s. In 1877 the Half-Dime Library was introduced with series including the character Deadwood Dick, whose adventures ran through thirty-three novels until his unfortunate death. Readers' demands forced the quick appearance of Deadwood Dick Jr., whose adventures ran through another sixty-three issues. Other popular characters included Dick Doom, Dandy Rock, and Buffalo Bill, the latter featured in a series of one hundred novels in the Dime and Half-Dime Library formats.

Whether his wife's death in 1889 influenced Beadle's decision to retire is unclear, but that year he decided to return permanently to Cooperstown, where he had spent each summer for many years. His youngest son, Walter, had died sometime earlier. Beadle was sixty-eight years of age in 1889 and a millionaire. During the next five years he stayed at his estate east of Cooperstown, which he had purchased in 1880 and named Glimmerview. He died there on 18 December 1894.[32]

NOTES

1. Walter J. Beadle, *Samuel Beadle Family: History and Genealogy of Decedents of Samuel Beadle, Planter Who Lived in Charlestown, Massachusetts in 1656 and Died in Salem, Massachusetts in 1664* (Privately published, 1970), 791.

2. John A. Garraty and Mark C. Carnes, eds., *American National Biography*, vol. 2 (New York: Oxford University Press, 1999), 392. See also *The National Cyclopaedia of American Biography*, vol. 19 (New York: James T. White, 1967; reprint, Ann Arbor MI: University Microfilms, 1967), 125.

3. Garraty and Carnes, *American National Biography*, 2:392.

4. Garraty and Carnes, *American National Biography*, 2:392.

5. Beadle, *Samuel Beadle Family*, 791.

6. The best history of the publishing career of Beadle is Albert Johannsen,

*The House of Beadle and Adams and Its Dime and Nickel Novels: The Story of a Vanished Literature*, 3 vols. (Norman: University of Oklahoma Press, 1950–62).

7. James C. Olson and Ronald C. Naugle, *History of Nebraska*, 3d ed. (Lincoln: University of Nebraska Press, 1995), 91–92.

8. Olson and Naugle, *History of Nebraska*, 87.

9. Olson and Naugle, *History of Nebraska*, 92.

10. Governor Mark W. Izard, "Opening Message to the Third Session of the Legislative Assembly, January 3, 1857," in *Messages and Proclamations of the Governors of Nebraska, 1854–1941*, vol. 1 (Lincoln: Nebraska State Historical Society, 1941), 43.

11. Beadle last mentions the Trinity House Hotel on 23 April. In his diary entry of 31 May and thereafter he refers to it as the Central House.

12. Diary entry for Friday, 3 April.

13. From the *Nebraskian*, 22 October 1856, as quoted in Alfred I. Finlayson, *The Mysterious Disappearance of Saratoga* (unpublished manuscript, Douglas County Historical Society, Omaha), 9.

14. J. Sterling Morton and Albert Watkins, *Illustrated History of Nebraska*, vol. 2 (Lincoln: Jacob North and Company, 1905–13), 23.

15. Alfred T. Andreas, *History of the State of Nebraska*, vol. 1 (1882; reprint, Chicago: The Western Historical Society, 1995), 778.

16. In his diary entry for 6 April Beadle mistakenly refers to Experience Estabrook as attorney general, a title and role with which he was probably familiar in New York state. As a territory Nebraska did not have an office of attorney general. Estabrook was appointed in 1854 by President Franklin Pierce as U.S. attorney for Nebraska Territory.

17. From the *Nebraskian*, 22 October 1856, as quoted in Finlayson, *Mysterious Disappearance*, 9–10; see also Ann L. Wilhite, *Books, Bibles, and Boosters: Colleges on the Urban Frontier of Nebraska Territory 1854–1867* (thesis, Creighton University, 1977), 165.

18. From the *Nebraskian*, 22 October 1856, as quoted in Finlayson, *Mysterious Disappearance*, 9–10.

19. Garneth O. Pearson, Susan L. Ruby, and Martin Shukert, *A Comprehensive Program for Historic Preservation in Omaha* (Omaha: Klopp Printing Co., 1980), 16. The body of water known today as Carter Lake was a section

of the Missouri River known as Saratoga Bend in 1857. It was a part of the Missouri until the river cut a new channel following a flood in 1877, leaving the bend separated from the river and creating the lake.

20. Olson and Naugle, *History of Nebraska*, 88–90.

21. Olson and Naugle, *History of Nebraska*, 83.

22. Addison E. Sheldon, *Nebraska: The Land and the People*, vol. 1 (Chicago: Lewis Publishing Co., 1931), 241.

23. Morton and Watkins, *Illustrated History*, 1:256.

24. Andreas, *History of the State*, 1:719.

25. Morton and Watkins, *Illustrated History*, 1:309.

26. Morton and Watkins, *Illustrated History*, 2:23.

27. Morton and Watkins, *Illustrated History*, 2:26.

28. Morton and Watkins, *Illustrated History*, 2:31. See also Andreas, *History of the State*, 1:693.

29. Finlayson, *Mysterious Disappearance*, 22.

30. Johannsen, *The House*, 1:26.

31. Johannsen, *The House*, 1:319.

32. A Beadle family biography can be found in the Beadle Family Papers at the New York Public Library Rare Books and Manuscripts Division.

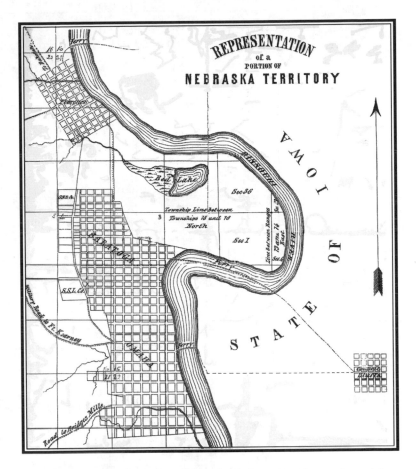

Map 1. Representation of a portion of Nebraska Territory, 1857. Cartographer and date unknown. Historical Society of Douglas County, gift of Charles Martin.

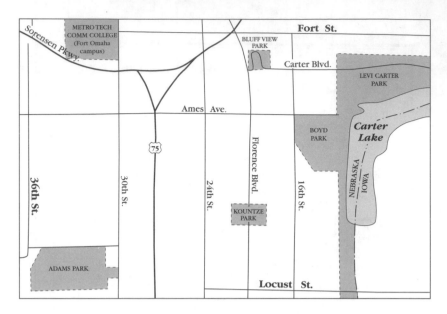

Map 2. The area of present-day Omaha that once was Saratoga.

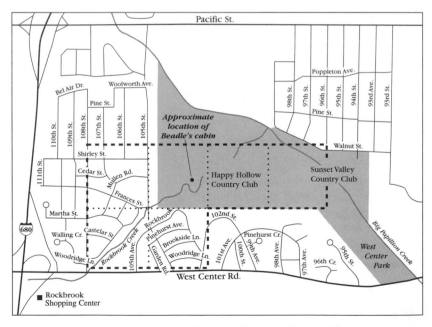

Map 3. The approximate location of Erastus F. Beadle's claim,
Rock Brook Farm, on a present-day map of Omaha.

# The Diary

*March 9th 1857* — Left home with the intention of being absent longer than any previous trip I had ever taken from my own fireside. Still I had none of those feelings which usually possess me at parting with my nearest and dearest of friends and relatives. I had no realizing sence of any protracted absence more than I would feel on going to my daily business. Days previous to my departure however were days of deep thought and reflection. The simplest acts of my children were unusually interesting to me and remarks that at any other time I would barely notice would make my heart swell and tears start unbidden in my eyes. But when the day for my departure arrived I was suffering with bodily ills of a more serious nature than I was willing to own and my mind was wholly occupied with those ills which were at the time painfull in the extreme. With as little ceremony as possible I bid goodby to my family and rode down to the depot chatting by the way with Irwin who "wanted to ride down with father." He was so taken up with his ride he was not inclined to get out of the sleigh and when I had bought my ticket and looked around to bid him good-by he was not to be found. He had remained in the sleigh where I found him bundled up playing the owner of the sleigh, as large as any one. I asked him if he was not going to bid me good-by? "Oh yes!" he says and the words he would have uttered in addition choked in his throat. He kissed me and when I had got a few feet from the sleigh he said Good-bye Pa! with a force to it I could but notice as coming from a full heart.

Only a short time was occupied in reaching and crossing the ferry at

Black Rock and getting under way on the Canada Side. The excitement of changing at Black Rock from cars to boat and boat to cars, had the effect to exhaust me considerable. For me at least, We were fortunate, in having but few passengers. I monopolized two whole seats near the stove and slept some before we reached Paris. At Paris we made the connection with the Great Western Cars. By the time we had reached London I began to regret my having left home in the condition I did. Continued to get sicker until about four o'clock p.m. when my feelings changed as if by Magic and I felt like a new being, ate a hearty supper on the boat crossing from Windsor to Detroit, and except from weakness and lassitude felt as well as I ever did in my life.

At Detroit called on Mr. Frazer who gave me a pass to Michigan City. Got a seat in the cars near the stove. Left at 9.20 and slept some of the way to Marshal.

*Tusday 10th*  Walked from the Depot up to the Marshal House and went to bed a three o'clock A. M. Slept but little, at seven breakfasted and soon after got a buggy from the livery to take me up four Miles on the plank. Had a pleasant but cold ride, found cousin's family all well. Cousin Joel Mack has a fine farm of 160 acres a good large frame house and is very comfortably situated, has a family of six children the two oldest boys who are married and living away by themselves the two next daughters one 20 and the other 16 years of age, a boy 13 and the baby a girl of five years completes his list of children. His daughter of 16 is the largest of the children is a perfect picture of My Sister Sybil when I last saw her and the baby is just another such a person as was Sister Emily at her age. The more I saw them the more I saw a resemblance both in looks and actions, but I do not believe Abigail the one resembling Sybil will live long she has a hard cough which I believe will prove fatal. My stay at Cousin Joels was a pleasant one. Cousin is a great speller and gramarian is a boy with his children and joins in their studies. His Wife is just such a farmers wife as others I have seen.

The Most interesting member of the family however was Aunt Abigail. In most respects she bears her eighty-five winters remarkably well, in walking she uses a cain and stands in a stooping position exactly as does Mrs. Hodge. She will weigh about 175 lbs. her weight in health was 200. She some resembles Uncle Chauncy in feature, but she has the eyes and nose of My father. I spent the day wholly with her most agreeably and instructive. She would ask me many questions about my Uncles and Aunts, and in a few hours ask much the same questions. Then she would remember she had asked before and received the same answer. When I informed her that all her Mothers and first step mothers children were dead she would remark with tears and a trembling voice "Yes they are *all gone* not one of my old acquaintance is living all are in their graves and *why* am *I* left? Yes and I have buried *two* husbands and eight of my ten children." She could not speak of the past without tears, not even of the days when she was a little girl and went to the village school of Colchester Con. which was about a half mile from her fathers house and Shop. When she spoke of the death of her first stepmother she wept like a child. She was the only Mother she ever knew and was one of the best of Mothers to her. "A few days before she died" says Aunt "She nursed Flavel then but ten Months old, kissed him and handed him to me and said she should never nurse him again, gave him to me as my child and said I must have him sleep with me and be kind and good to him for he never would know what it was to have a Mother to care for him and I always felt he was my child." When Aunt told this she would manifest as much grief as she could have done the day her Mother died. Her grief was monitory as that of a child.

Her bodily health and apetite is as good as it ever was and she can eat as wholesome food, she is but very little care, occupies her own corner with her own chair and table she used when young eats by herself and lives within herself, reads but little except her bible that is her all. She read over the old family Record of uncle James a number of times and expressed no little surprise she should have remembered her own age. She was pleased to have me ask her for her degareotype but said she had no money to get it taken with but would go up and sit for it had never had one taken.

*Wednesday 11*  Slept comfortably last night and for the first time in years between woollen sheets in the regular oldfashioned style. After a late breakfast Cousin harnessed to a cutter we helped Aunt in and started for Marshal. Cousin was the first setler where he now lives, his team made the first waggon track where now the planck road runs. The vicinity is thickly settled with wealthy farmers and fine farm buildings.

Aunt bore her ride well walked up and down stairs without assistance. The artist who took her picture does not understand his business and made a picture I did not fancy. If Mr. Evans had had such a subject he would have done it justice but a poor opperator a poor subject poor tools poor stock alltogether what more could be expected.

When all was ready to start, Aunt comfortably seated in the sleigh, she took hold of me to bid me good bye and thank me for having her picture taken. She said "When you write to your mother and your wife and children remember me with love to them, remember me to my brothers and sisters living and Erastus *remember your Creator!*" Aunt has been a very intelligent woman for her time or for the times in which she has lived. I wish I could be where she was a month.

Leaving the deguerrean room I went to the depot learned that the cars had run off the track and were three hours behind time did not get away until Six P. M. and reached Michigan City at a little past eleven the same night, but 20 Minutes too late for the Cars the next train was to leave the next day at ten A. M. I accordingly went to the Jewell house and to bed.

On leaving Marshall a Novelty presented itself, in the form of a little boy about Irwin's age and hight but more chubby he followed the business of making speeches on the cars and then passing around his hat. He understood the business to perfection. When he first commenced his hat off and his hair brussled up I thought him crazy but soon discovered my mistake. He had a powerful voice and could controll it like an orritor every one could here him in the car and the speed was 30 miles an hour. A new way to raise the wind.

*Thursday 12*  A clear and stinging cold morning. Time hanging heavily I walked out to see the town as soon as the sun was up sufficiently to warm the atmosphere. Michigan City is in Indiana on the shoar of Lake Michigan is the Junction of the new Albany and Salem R. R. is a fine place for a town but can never amount to much, as a city. It is somewhat protected from the winds of the lake by very high bluffs rising near two or three hundred feet. These bluffs have some shrubberry and scattering oaks, and covered with sand from the lake which is thrown up in drifts by the high and almost constant blowing wind. The present covering of the bluffs is composed of about equal parts of snow and sand, and this morning was froze as hard as ice still I succeeded in reaching the top of the highest bluf by pulling myself up by the shrubs and crawling on my hands and knees in real *Mount blanc* style. From the top of the bluff I could see for one hundred miles in all directions and could easily imagine myself one of the daring adventurers of *Mt. Blanc* itself on a small scale.

The time passed as casily as I could expect and at 10.10 A. M. I left on the cars in a direct South course. For the first ninety miles the country was mostly prarrie and wet at that, and the most untractible country I ever saw it is a "Hoosier" state in earnest. The buildings were nothing but the poorest kind of logg huts, and unless you saw some *human* animals you would not think they were inhabited, all they raise is corn and pork. This also constitutes their sole diet spiced with the "*shakes*" without which they think they could not live they make as much calculations about having the shakes fall and spring as they to to have the seasons themselves come and go in fact they coud not live if they did not have the shakes half the time. Whole fields of corn were only cut up and stood out all winter, on account of the shakes taking them too soon in many places they were drawing in their corn.

Near many of the logg huts, some of which were deserted I noticed small enclosures formed by driving short stakes in the ground a few inches apart and but two or three feet high. These varied in size from ten to one hundred feet square. Internally they presented no different appearance from the immediate vicinity which convinced me they were not gardens. On inquiry I was told they were graveyards. Many of which contained whole familys. These yards were usually in a few rods of the house and in many locations were the only show of improvement or civilization.

Every hours progress we made we could see we was fast leaving the vicinity of snow, and when we reached Lafayette at 3.30 P. M. there was but very little snow to be seen. About 2 oclock we saw black birds and Meadow larks and soon after leaving Lafayette large flocks of prairie hens.

At 7 P. M. we reached Indianapolis where we were obliged to wait until Eleven P. M. before starting for Cincinnati. This evening was a delightful one not cold enough to require winter over coats and seemed like an April night at home.

*Friday 13* Reached Cincinnati five o'clock this Morning and put up at the "Burett House" had an early breakfast made a scedule of my business for the day and at nine o'clock had all my business that called me to Cincinnati done. Got My boots by Express from Buffalo found them too large by two or three sizes so I am almost bootless.

Nine o'clock commenced searching for James Pennington searched all day but withous success. A marked change in the atmosphere between this place and where I was yesterday morning. There was good sleighing and the thermometer near Zero here they were wattering broadway to keep down dust.

Cincinnati at this season of the year is remarkably brisk the principal exports I saw was whisky pork and ready made buildings which is a great business here. The levee is litteraly crowded with boxes, barrels, carts drays &c and every steamer crowding on freight altogether it is the busyest place I ever saw.

At five oclock P. M. Took passage on board the steam Packet Memphis bound for Memphis and Hickman Tenn. The officers of the boat protested against the large amount of freight the proprietors put on, as there was but a little over five feet water on the bars and the boat was loaded down to a draught of near seven feet. In this state we left at ten o'clock at night soon after I had retired.

*Saturday 14* Had made good headway during the night but about ten o'clock A. M. when within 20 miles of Louisville we grounded, and remained there until ten at night. Could only get off by getting two flat boats and taking out some one hundred ton to lighten her. These flat boats are kept along the river for this purpose and are called lighters. The bed of the Ohio is hard gravel and a boat can not work off as on the sand bars of the Missouri. We have a variety of passengers some fifty in all mostly Southerners they all take me for a Southerner. We have a "Nigger" trader on board.

*Sunday 15* — A delightfull day. More like the Middle of May in Buffalo than the 15th of March. It has been a day of anxious watching for Captain crew and passengers, as the barge from Cincinnati has been hourly expected but has failed to reach us. I have walked over the principal parts of the City in Company with a young man from Philadelphia. Louisville like Cincinnati presents a very dingy appearance owing to burning so much coal. The Streets are wide and well supplied with shade trees which are much needed in the summer which are very warm here. Towards Evening we walked up in the vicinity of the best residence which was quite a treat to Me doors and windows were thrown open, and Ladies were out on the steps and balconies with nothing on their heads, and dressed in late spring dresses. It was in great contrast with the previous Sunday in Buffalo which was like mild winter.

We saw during the day a number of funerals. The hearses in use here are glazed on both sides and ends rendering the coffin wholly visible. The Hearse is painted black and trimed with silver on the sides the top is ornamented with four clusters of Prince of Wales plumes on each side. It is altogether quite a showy vehicle and is used for the poor classes as well as the rich.

Louisville has a large number of coulered people about 3000 of which are slaves. They are probably cared better for than any city in the Union.

*Monday 16* — Last evening was very pleasantly spent in the Cabin. We have a large number of passengers mostly Southerners a fair proportion of Ladies all of which could sing and play on the piano. We had a sociable time. Those of us that were married showed the degareotypes of our wives and children. I took the premium. They said they look like Northerners, supposing I was a Southerner. They said they were *"right fine"* looking and a *"heap* prettier" than I was. I knew they only wanted to flatter me and took it for what it was worth.

An affray took place in the forward cabin on Saturday Night that came near resulting in the loss of life. The parties were from Mississipi were engage in card playing until a late hour and drinking freely used their revolvers and bowie knives. They think no more of shooting at each other than the people North do of taking a round with the fist.

I got acquainted with a number of gentlemen from the South some merchants others professional men. They were extremely warm hearted. They consider the use of the revolver as honorable a way of settling a dispute or punishing an insult as any plan that can be adopted. The strong Man has not there the advantage. It is their education and they succeed in making out a quite a case in their favor.

On going to bed last evening we were in hopes to be on our way again before morning as the barge was still expected. Morning came however and we were still at the levee in Louisville. My patience was exhausted. This was the day we was to have been in Memphis, and now the Captain told us it would take three to four days after the barge came to get to Memphis. I went up town after breakfast and found I could take the cars to St. Louis one dollar less than at Cincinnati. I returned to the boat and the Captain refunded all of my passage money except $2.50. So that it cost me only $1.50 extra to go by Louisville. Many of the passengers left the boat as I did while others remained. I should have remained if I could have spared the time as I never was on a steamer where they lived as well as they did on the Memphis. The boat is noted for the table it sets.

At Noon there was no news from the barge. The R. R. omnibuss called at the boat for me took me to the ferry thence to the depot of the New Albany and Salem R. R. and at 1.50 P. M. We left, reached Greencastle behind time but the cars waited five minutes enabling us to get aboard. Changed cars again at Terre Haute and Vincenes.

*Tuesday 17.* — From Vincenes reached Sandoval about Eight o'clock A. M. Found no Cars to Centralia until one in the afternoon. I accordingly checked My baggage to Centralia and started on foot the distance Six Miles. I found it a very pleasant walk indeed. Most of the way was prairie. One grove however of about one mile was a pleasant variety. It was filled with birds which made me halt a number of times to listen to the variety of noises they made. Among the number was a Mocking bird and the Cardinal Grosebeak or Red Bird. Neither of them get as far North as New York. I have seen No robins yet.

I came in Sight of Centralia when about two Miles distant from the town. My imagination located Harriets residence and all of the particulars. I had it in the south east part of the village on the open prarie without a yard fence or any thing of the Kind. When near enough to distinguish the buildings I selected one, a Story and a half white house with two conspicuous side windows visible one and a half miles off. That is the place I remarked aloud and laughed heartily all to myself. I ploded on into the heart of the town, at the depot I inquired where Hugh Baily lived. Was informed that it was in the 'Coponys Row' a little east. Next enquired at a Stoor and was pointed out the very house I had selected on first coming in sight of the town. I shall have to believe in Spiritualism I think after this. Entered Harriets house as familiar as though I belonged there, and without nocking. I believe she jumped some and seemed pleased to see Me. They are living as comfortable as can be considering the house is not finished. Baily soon came in to dinner and was heartily glad to see me. I left with him at two o'clock and rode on his engine down to Cairo got there at 8 P. M. Tried to get passage to Memphis but found the fare $10. I backed out sudden. Supposed it but $8. Got into the mud up to my knees. Went with Mr. Baily to bed.

*Wednesday 18* — Left Cairo on my return with Mr. Baily at 6 A. M. Reached Centralia at Noon. Set by the fire. Visited and played with the baby during the balance of the day.

*Thursday 19* — A warm and pleasant day. Baily drawed fence lumber and had his garden ploughed. I walked about the Town. Wrote and slept some and got well rested. Centralia is more of a town than I expected to find. Has some 1500 population. Harriet has a fine baby as any one has. Its hair is red and I believe always will be. It has a bad cold and I fear threatened with the croop. Mr. Baily and Hat. would not hear to my leaving under a week at least, and seemed dissatisfied when I decided to leave the next day. I fared sumptuously. Had a pressing invitation to have my family come out and stop a month or even three of them before going West.

*Friday 20* — Left Centralia half past twelve at night. Hat. set up and had a breakfast ready for me and Mr. Baily as he had to go out to Cairo again at two o'clock. Left the baby very poorly.

Harriet Keeps a girl a big dog and hens. I think if any one takes comfort it is them. They are as loving as two kittens.

We reached St. Louis between five and six in the Morning. At The Barnum House I found a letter from Frank and Robert Adams but very much to my surprise not a line from wife or children. After breakfast went down to the boats. No boats were going further up than St. Joseph. Ice reported 30 inches thick at Omaha and teams crossing. This presented a dubious aspect. I had hurried to get away and hurried all the way and here I am two weeks too early. This gave me the blues a little and I Knew not what course to pursue. In this dillema I went in search of my Cousin. Found two brothers of Cousin Benjamin. They were Alfred and James H. The former has a wife and nine children. James has a wife but has lost all his children. He is two years younger than I am. Took dinner and went up to supper and spent a short time in the evening.

Returning to My Hotel I had decided to go back to Harriets and stop a week or ten days until the ice was out of the river and I could get a passage to Omaha. With this determination I went to bed.

*Saturday 21* — Arose early, examined the register of arrivals and found the name of G. W. Brown of Laurence. He had come in the afternoon previous from Chicago but was not yet up. I took breakfast and then went to his room. And our meeting was decidedly a joyous to both. He insisted on my going to Laurence With him and make his house my home until I could take passage up the river. His wife would be in from Alton in time to go out with us. I accordingly abandoned going back to Harriets, and set about making preparations to accompany Mr Brown into Kansas. At 2 P. M. we left in the Cars for Jefferson City where we were to meet the R. R. Company's daily line of steamers for Weston and intermediate points. Our tickits taking us through.

Our party from St. Louis consisted of Mr Brown and his wife, A Mrs. Leavett and her two daughters ten and six years of age. We had a very pleasant time on the cars. Mr. Brown Fathered one of Mrs. L.'s children and I took Mrs Brown under My care. Mrs. Leavett and family were among the number that were driven out of Leavenworth last summer, and lost all they had. They are now located at Wyandot, where Mr. Leavett now is. Mrs. L. is going out to Join him. Mrs. Leavett is one of the fire brands of the freestates party. Her tongue is constantly busy. She has been east Making speeches and getting Subscribers for Mr Browns paper. She has become desperate and if necessity requires it she will take up the muskett and revolver before she will be again driven away from her home. She is ready for an argument with any one even on spiritualism. Mrs Brown is a more quiet woman and looks like a person that has been tried as she has been.

We were informed at St Louis that the two boats were usually crowded, so that when the whistle blew at Jefferson City every person had their carpet sack in hand to make a spring for the boat when the cars should stop. And when they did stop down they went in a mass like a flock of sheep tumbling over each other in the dark, (it was eight o'clock at night). But lo and behold not a berth stool or plank was unoccupied. The daily boats due were aground up the river, and the one in, the *New Lucy* had been damaged and could not leave until the next day in the afternoon when her damages would probably be repaired. No boat had been in for three days that belonged to the line and two trains of cars per day loaded as thick as they could stand, had poured into the city, and as soon as the New Lucy reached her landing she was swarmed and every room taken. Our chances were to hang up on a hook. Finding the Capt. he proved to be no less a person than the Pilot of the *Wm. Campbell* the boat I came down on last fall. He recognized me at once and fixed out two rooms which were given up to the Ladies and Mr Brown. Next in Order Mr. Brown and Myself went up town to get supper. Not having dinner we felt the want of supper. We set down to a table. That was about all. Got a cup of cold coffee a small biscuit one cracker and that was *all*. Charges only *50 cents each*. Returning to the boat Mr Brown Made a miss step and tumbled into a gulph about five feet deep with a Mud bottom, tore his clothes some and hurt him a little, but not sufficient to prevent us from laughing heartily. We scraped mud for some time then he ventured on the boat. I walked in front to screen him from to conspicuous a view. When readhing the ladies cabin we quickend our pace again. Mr Brown met with a casualty. Run his head against one of the branches of the chandelier. Nocked off the globe smashing it in a thousand pieces. Every eye was turned in the direction. There he stood watching the fragments and covered with mud. A more ludicrus scene I have seldom beheld and if he had killed himself I could not help but laugh. He got into his room and there remained for the night.

About this time the porters comenced turning down the chairs along along the state room doors completely blocking up the entrance or exits through the door. This being done they brough in a lot of Mattresses arranging them along one end on the chair backs to serve as a pillow. I took the hint and made fast to one. Then came a general strife to see who should have a bed. About one half were accommodated. Some had a mattress some a pillow others a blanket. Covering about two thirds of cabin floor, one would laugh another sing and a third curse, those that could get no chance to sleep done all they could to prevent others from sleeping and kickt up a general uproar until they got exhausted and we at last got to sleep. I was soare from laughing at the vanity of disposition, one was for fun another kept up a constant growl. Those however who said least fared best. I have often heard people tell of a crowd, but this beat all.

*Sunday 22* — This morning another amusing scene was enacted which will probably be repeted three times per day during the trip. There are three hundred passengers on board and only table room for some Seventy five. Who was to be first at table was the all engrossing Subject as soon as preparations were commenced for breakfast. It was with difficulty that the waiters could get around to put the dishes on the tables. I saw at once that those without ladies must of necessity fare slim. I accordingly secured Mrs. Leavett for meal times which was for me very fortunate. The table had to be cleared and set again four times before all the passengers were served. The fare is of the poorest kind I ever saw on a steamboat even at the first tables. Females were in great demand at meal times even little girls that went free were engaged for the trip in order to secure a seat at the first table. We have two large and very amusing men by the name of Martin from Flint Mich who are brothers. They take girls of 11 and 9 years to the table as their ladies. We are all becoming acquainted and are anticipating a pleasant time. On showing my degareotypes Mr Martin recollected seeing Mate somewhere. It was at Flint. This is how I became acquainted with him, he knows Lib. and Cook. He says Mrs. Cook is one of the finest women in Flint and has the most Friends of any one in the city and that I ought to be proud of her sister for a wife.

Mr. Brown and myself have had a stroll about the city. The town does not amount to much except as the Capital of Mo. Our boat was repaired about noon but we were obliged to wait until the three o'clock cars came in as one of the pilots had gone down to St. Louis. Our steam was up ready to start as soon as the pilot should come on board so as to prevent the rush of passengers from the train. They came however like an avalanche covering our forecastle as thick as they could stand. They were ordered off on another boat of the same line going out the next day. Among the crowd of new comers I saw and spoke with three Buffalo men, Lawyer Grey Mr. Metz and a young man whom I cannot call by name. Was once a clerk at Calendars.

During the day I have made the acquaintance of a Mr Smith who together with his wife is going to Omaha to establish themselves in business. He is a small man about the size of Mr. Cook and of the same business. His wife is a very tall woman, reminds me of Mrs. Newman. She is a graduate of some of our eastern seminaries and has herself been for a term of years a principal. She hopes to be enabled to establish an institution of learning at Omaha. I think she would be just the woman for such an enterprise. I shall use my influence. I should be ready then to take my family to Omaha.

On the arrival of the cars which brought up our pilot, this Mr. Smith went up to look after some baggage which came on the train. He succeeded in getting the baggage nearly to the boat when it put out, and would not return. You may imagine the feelings of his wife who was obliged to remain on this boat while her husband must stop over a day and come on the next boat. There are a number on this boat going to Omaha some of which will stop with her at Weston until her husband arrives.

Some seven miles above Jefferson City is the worst sand-bar on the route and as we expected or feared we got fast on it in company with other boats some had been there 48 hours, this was not a very pleasant prospect for us. We made the best of it however and concluded too sleep on it. This night I succeeded in getting a state room in company with Mr. Carver of Buffalo. (He is the man with whom Desdimona boarded.) He had a room for himself and his two sons, his two sons slept together giving me a birth to myself which I appreciate. I could not retire until I had seen the sport in the Main cabin of staking or marking out claims and securing a place to straiten out in for the night. This evening we had a fine thunder shower.

*Monday 23* — Early this morning one of the Steamers on the barr, the "Star of the West" got off and passed up. Soon after this the "Col. Crossman" which left St. Louis the day before we did, and which we passed on the cars, came up and crossed the barr without difficulty cheering loudly as they passed us. The "Crossman" stoped a Mile up to wood. In the mean time we came up along side of them to wood also. In swinging around we came in collission with the Crossman and smashed in our wheelhouse on the same side the previous injury was sustained. Again we were disable, and when the Crossman left we lashed to the shoar for repairs where we remained in an uneasy state of axiety until after eight o'clock at night.

The early part of the day was rainy. The afternoon was dry and pleasant. The scenery on the shore grand. Mr. Brown and myself invited some ladies to attempt to gain the top of a rock which we had been admiring all the day. It is by far the loftiest rock I have yet seen. It towred far above the loftiest trees. On the side next the river it was perpendicular over 200 feet high and scalloped out like a chimney and for want of a better name we called it "Chimney rock." We ascended by climbing up the bank which in the rear of the rock extended to within 50 feet of the top. We then got up one at a time to a secure foothold and pulled the others after us, reaching the top we gave three cheers for *free Kansas*. Fifty persons could stand upon the top of the rock, our company consisted of some eight or ten. I did not venture to look off at the brink as others did, at first I was too timid to stand erect. We gathered some moss as relics and carved our names in the rock and on the limbs of trees along the side of the path by which we ascended. We all agreed that our visit to the top of "Chimney rock" had well paid us for the delay we were subjected to by the accident to our boat.

When I took the cars at Sandoval on Friday morning at one o'clock, every seat was occupied. Noticing a gentleman whose countenance pleased me, I asked and received a share of his seat. We conversed most of the way to St Louis. His manner of speaking was exceedingly pleasant and he bore a striking resemblance to Uncle Chauncy except he was not corpulent his height is Six feet six inches, and he is one of the noblest looking men I ever saw. He was an old resident of Missouri. I was exceedingly loth to part with him as I did at the ferry opposite St. Louis, and equally pleased to meet him again at "The Barnum House." In the afternoon of the same day I again met him on the levvy as he was about to take the cars for Jefferson City *en route* home. We parted here as old friends neither knowing the others name. On Sunday Morning at Jefferson City we again met. He had been waiting for the boat to be repaired. Was stoping in the city with his daughter, was going up on the same boat, had with him a niece and a little slave he was taking up to a friend and neighbor of his.

I think I have never met with a man that pleased me as well. I also think I have learned much that will be of service to me in the way of business in the West. My friend's name is Samuel C. Major is one of the wealthy and most prominent men of Missouri.

This evening Mr Major and Myself were called upon by the ladies, who had held a meeting and voted to invite the Captain and Clerk to visit them in the ladies Cabin, with a deposition from said ladies to transmit the vote to the Captain, which we did, feeling flattered by the compliment, and reported favorable. This involved the necessity of an introduction which could only be done in general terms as we were not acquainted with but few of the ladies on board, by Name. The evening passed pleasantly, with another thunder shower to close the day. At nine o'clock a dive was made for the mattress, claims taken, and in the general melee, in which some got kick and and scratches we went to bed. Our friend was obliged to stretch his six feet six on the Cabin floor. Something *he* was not used to.

*Tuesday 24* — But little progress made during the night. My friend

Major pointed out the burial place of *Daniel Boon* and told me that his niece on the boat was a Great Grand Daughter of Daniel Boon, as yet I had not spoken with her. I asked an introduction, which was given with an apology that it had not been done before. I concidered it a great treat to be in conversation with a direct decendent of the "*old Hunter of Kentucky.*" Miss Boon is a woman of intelligence and education of a high order, born and brought up in Missouri. She seems to inherit a large share of that love for the wildness of nature that charactiresed her Grandsire. She had learned from her Uncle that I was from the state of New York. She asked me many questions about the scenery of N. Y. particularly that of Niagara, St Lawrence, Lake George the Hudson and the scenery described by Cooper. She had only visited the part of Kentucky where her Great Grandfather lived, and a small portion of Tenessee. She would talk of wild scenery different from any one I ever conversed with. And I regret I did not make her acquantonce earlier. She and her Uncle left the boat this Morning at Eleven. On leaving the boat they bade me a friendly good bye wishing me a pleasant journy and asking to be remembered to my wife and children whose likeness they saw.

The water in the river has been rising slowly to day and our progress is rapid for Missouri traveling. Wild geese are in great Abundance. The shores and sand-bars are covered by the thousands. The air is becoming more chilly.

*Wednesday 25* — The watter continues to rise in the river. We passed the Col. Crossman about one o'clock this morning and are fast making up for our delay in repairing the boat. About 8 o'clock we came upon a deer that was on a sand-bar. He made quick steps in the direction of the nearest timber land taking to the water part of the way.

After dinner we passed the "Star of the West" that passed us while on the bar Monday Morning. She left St. Louis three days in advance of us. We are the fastest craft on the river and pass everything afloat. About this time the Porter came around ordering those stoping at Kansas City to Select their baggage. This was the first intimation we had of our coming to the vicinity of our seperation. We had been jamed into our cabin like stage coach passengers and most of us had become acquainted and I presume our seperation was much as it is on ship board after a long and perrilous voyage. Our passengers were from all parts of the Union but mostly from Western New York, among our passengers was an officer of the Steam Ship Baltic who had been on her every trip since she was built. He is so taken up with our Western country he has almost determined to locate her. He had no idea such people went to Kansas. Mr. Brown hired two printers and one young lady to go and work for him at Lawrence. He made Me liberal offers. I told him I must first try Omaha. He would pay me my price if I would go with him. He is coining money. Has 7000 subscribers. The greater part of our passengers were bound for Kansas and mostly for Lawrence and vicinity. All of the Kansas Emigrants they charged extra on their baggage weighing every piece. The Nebraska passengers were allowed to go on with all they had a mind to. I must say I think the best persons on the boat were among the Nebraska passengers. We reached Kansas City Mo. about Eleven at night when we parted with some 40 or 50 of our passengers. A few miles further on is Wyandot where Mrs Leavett family and others got off. By this time the favored ones got rooms for the balance of the night.

A blackleg traveling on the boat was a nuesence. He swindled some two hundred dollars out of different persons that played with him. One young man lost thirty dollars all he had and then offered to pawn his watch. This was told to me. I did not see it feeling more at home in the ladies cabin. I spent most of the time there. During the evening this blackleg insulted a man who was about getting off. He called him to an account and challenged him to shoot with him on the hurrycain deck. Arrangements were being made and I had made up my mind to see the thing done. I could have seen the blackleg shot down with as good grace as I would shoot a chicken if I was hungry. It would have been doing a blessed cervice for the county. The friends of the rascal settled the difficulty.

I have become acquainted with J. Johnson of the Johnson House N.Y. City. He is going to Omaha with a view of erecting a fine hotel if every thing suits him. He is a fine man. None of your swelling bragadasius but a true gentleman. He will be a worthy and useful acqui- to Omaha should he take up his residence there.

*Thursday 26*  The watter still rising is three feet higher than when we left Jefferson City Sunday Night. Wild Turkeys were seen running along the banks on the Missouri side this morning.

A short time after breakfast We reached Leavenworth City. The levee was completely Swarmid with people before we landed. So much so that the two hundred passengers we landed did not seem to enlarge the crowd in the least. Here I met my friend Kellum from Auban who went west when I was last at Auburn. His company were waiting for a through boat to continue on as far as Omaha. I learned there were no accommodations at Leavenworth or Lawrence so I decided to work my way along and get to Omaha the best way possible.

The clerk of our boat says that since the river has opened there has 12,000 people passed up in boats for Kansas and Nebraska and as many more by land. Every ferry we came to was crowded from Morning to Night. Such a tide of emigration was never before known. They are pouring in one continual stream to every town and ferry on the east bank of the river and stand in large groops of men, women, children, waggons, horses and oxen awaiting their turn to cross into the promise land. They tell us they are only pioneers and have but to write home favorable to bring parties of from ten to twenty for every individual now entering the Territories. They are covering the territories like a swarm of locusts. The border-ruffian population of Missouri shak their heads and heep curses upon the Yankies. "Their curses like little chickens will come to roost." Missourie must and will ere long become a free state.

Our stop at Leavenworth was but a few Moments. We reached Weston the terminus of the "Lightning Line" at ten o'clock. Stoped at the "St George Hotel." The stage to St. Josephs had gone, three extras were hired, and filled with some twenty-five, myself among the number agreed to wait for a boot. The day spent in writing and prospecting about the town. It is a mistery to me why a town was ever built on the site of Weston. There is not a dozen houses in the place on a level with each other. So uneven is the ground that houses on the same street 300 feet apart of equal size will vary fifty feet in height. During rain storms the ground washes very bad so that the ravines can not be bridged and deep gulphs are cut out by the rain to the level of the river. No watter runs in these gullies except during the rainstorm, still they are impossible. The city reminds me of pictures I have seen of towns in Switzerland.

Among the guests at the St. George was a gentleman and his wife from York state. Their respective ages were about 35 and 45 years. They belong to the better classes. They left their friends in the east with buoyant hopes and a light hearts for a "Home in the West." Their *only child* was a spritely little girl twenty two months old, a perfect little fairy, in this little being was centered the affection and soul of its parents. She was their idol. No one but a parent can tell how she was loved! On the boat she took sick, had a cold on her lungs, got no relief. Took her from the boat to the hotel where the little innocence lingered a few days and died. The day previous to her death she put her arms around her mothers neck clasping with her whole strength her "dear Mama." Then smoothing her cheek with her little feverish hand Kissed her mother a number of times and bade her goodbye! Two days after this they burried her among strangers in a strange land. Oh! was not that heartrending? I took the case home, I could but mingle my sympathising tears with theirs. Had it been one or both of my children what would have been my feelings. May I ever be spared such afflictions, but if Come they must I pray for strength and fortitude for such a trial.

Previous to the burial the corps was dressed and placed in a natural position as though alive in the fathers arms, and an ambrotype taken. It is the finest thing I ever saw. One not knowing the facts would think the child was pretending to be asleep and could with difficulty keep from laughing.

*Friday 27* — Got up this Morning as soon as it was light. Went up on the highest bluff. Could see a steamer coming up nine miles down the river. The boat proved to be the "Star of the West" which we had passed two days previous. By the time we had breakfast she had reached the landing. We took passage for St Joseph the boat going no farther up than that point. The family who burried their child is on board. The Mother seems allmost heart broken. She says her greatest trial came when she left the hotel without her child.

On board the "Star of the West" we have much better fare than on the Railroad line and I would advise all persons coming west to avoid said line. It is a humbug. The indipendent boats set a first rate table have enough and are accommodating and gentlemanly. Among the places we touched at was Atchison the strong hold of proslavery in Kansas. This is the residence of Stringfellow and is one of the places we stoped at last fall during the Kansas excitement. I bought a copy of the "Squatter Sovereign." Edited and published by Stringfellow. The number I bought contained the validictory of Stringfellow in which he stated he had published at his own expense, the "Squatter Sovereign" for two years "for the purpose of arousing the South to the importance of Kansas as a Territory piculiarly adapted to Slave labor." . . . "did not embark in the embark in the enterprise with a view of profit, but solely to prevent Kansas from being Abolitionised." He resigns his labors to other hands who will make the paper purely Democratic sustaining the law and order party and advocating the doctrines of the National democracy. The same paper contains an invitation to setlers from all parts of the Union North as well as South to come and make homes among them. The entire tone of the paper is changed. The only hope the proslavery party now have is to force through a convention without submitting it to the people. This they do not believe they can do.

The River is almost out of its banks and the current very rappid which makes our progress very slow. The scenery increases in beauty as we ascend nearer to the Nebraska line. Many persons who are on their first trip up the "Big Muddy" are in extacis about the Country.

We reached St. Joseph about nine o'clock in the Evening. Found the Hotels filled and accommodations poor. The persons that came up on the Extras the day previous were in time to take the Steamer Admiral bound for Omaha, which left this Morning at ten o'clock. We felt disappointed and very much regreted we had not followed their example in taking an extra. Our only chance now is to take the stage. We hurried to the office, three of us but only two could get seats. These were taken by a man from the Bluff and Myself. Our Cleveland friend decided to run his chances. Paid our fare and to bed dreading our Stage ride the Next day. Time by stage we were told was 36 hours.

*Saturday 28* — During last night the Steamer Col. Crossman arrived bringing another supply of passengers for the Upper Missouri. There was at least 100 passengers for the Bluffs and Omaha and only a Nine passenger Coach to take them, running every other day. The Stage would take no baggage except a satchel a valise to each passenger. We were obliged to leave our trunks in the storehouse to be sent up on the first boat.

A little after eight we started at a snail pace up one bluff and down another tiping and pitching in all directions. One of our passengers was a Mr Jackson of the firm of Footte & Jackson of the Bluffs and Omaha. He did not reach St. Josephs until this morning when all Seats were taken. He bought off one of the passengers giving him ten dollars bonus for his seat. The fare was ten dollars, so that Mr Jackson paid twenty dollars.

We found the roads much better than we had anticipated, being dry except in the hollows between blufs. The day was as pleasant as could be. Nothing of special interest transpired until about two o'clock P. M. when the stage got set in a mud hole and the horses down. We all had business now unfastening the horses while the driver held them on his coach, and one Man at each horses head until they were seperately detatched and got out of the mud. Next we took down the fence got a chain and attached it to the tongue of the coach hitched the horses to the chain. The horses in the lot where they had good foothold. With rails pryed up the coach so that horses drew it out safe on dry land. After an hours delay we were again on the move. At four o'clock We Stoped to change horses at a place called Oregon where we ordered dinner. At this place I saw for the first time handbills posted up advertising a sale of negroes. They were the property of heirs and must be sold to settle up an estate. There are but few slaves in this part of Missouri, and a better country I never saw. It Can not be beat in the world. They raise fruit in great abundance, we have all the apples we want two for a penny.

Ham, Eggs and Corn Cake constituted our bill of fare. This being disposed of we started on, footing down and up hills which were very steep, in one of these pedestrian excursions we came to a large Cornfield where the old stalks were standing. It was about Sundown, the cornfield was alive with Wild Geese and ducks that were coming in to feed on young wheat which was just starting up and to roost. The ground was covered with them and the air filled with others hovering over. The noise made by their wings and their constant squaking was almost deafning and shook the ground like distant thunder. Their number could not be estimated. With suitable firearms or snares we could have filled the coach. They did not seam at all timid. What a place for sporting.

Soon after dark our driver stoped to water his horses. When he started again, by some carelessness he brought the leaders around so sudden as to break the tongue of the coach. Here was a "pretty Kittle of fish." We were fortunate in being opposite a farm house, where a lumber waggon was procured with a view of continuing our Journey. This proved to be to small and we were obliged to allow the driver to return with the two forward wheels to Oregon and have a new tongue made. This the driver assured us would be done so he could return by two o'clock next Morning. We accordingly took possession of the farm house which was built in regular Missouri style, of hewed loggs and double. Two houses about fifteen feet square and twelve to fifteen feet apart, with a roof extending from one to the other. One part was used for Cooking and Eating the chamber for the boys (Negroes) to sleep in. The other apartment was the family room containing two beds, the room had a large fireplace and was the only sitting room. I could not stand up in this room with my hat on. The chamber was still lower. Into this living room we all huddle *Eleven* in number. Our host a clever bullet-headed Kentuckyan said he would make us as comfortable as he could under the circumstances. Preliminaries being arranged we all went up stairs where four beds were arranged along the side of the house on the floor lengthwise. This gave us room enough for the six footers to lay their bodies on the bed while their feet extended out on the floor. When all were ensconsed we were Covered with all sorts of bedding. We packed in soldier or prison style forming a hollow square and in twenty minutes most of the number were sound asleep snoaring in so many different keys as to resemble the squakin of the Wild geese.

*Sunday 29* — Slept Soundly all last night. Got an early breakfast of Bacon, Eggs and Corn Cake served up by a couple of ebony gentlemen. Our driver did not return until 9 o'clock when we again started being delayed twelve hours.

At twelve Noon stoped at Jackson's Point, named after our passenger Jackson who once lived there. Here we got a first rate dinner of roast turky. Our next station was 27 miles distance and great fears were entertained of how we should cross the big Tarkeo River some sixteen miles distant. The Snow in northern Iowa was melting and the river was out of its banks covering the entire bottoms. Reaching the regular crossing our driver swam it with one of the horses and learned by the agent who was on the opposite side and came over with the driver that we must go back two miles take another route and cross lower down. We accordingly did so crossing the Main stream on a bridge then came *four Miles* of river bottoms where the water was from three feet to six inches in depth all the way. Some of the time the horses could with difficulty draw the coach. It was long after dark when we reached the bridge where we should have crossed but for the watter, our route to cross the river had taken us fifteen miles out of our way. I shall always remember Crossing the *Big Tarkeo*.

It was now four miles to our station being 36 our team had to go, one of the horses will probably never go it again as we believe he is used up. These last four miles was hilly and we walked much of the way, which was delightfull. The prairie was on fire in all dirictions, and presented a most Magnificent sight. The grass was dry and tall and a gentle wind blowing which kept the fire steadily marching on like an army of Soldiers. Sometimes a gust of wind would strike a section of the line of fire increasing the flame and hasting it along ahead of the main line then Continue along the line in wavey motions like the undulations of the sea. In many places our road crossed the fire when we could see to read in the coach. We Could see fires in all directions and as far as the eye could extend. I took a Match and set a fresh fire where the grass was long and dry, before we were out of sight it covered acres. It is a splendid sight in a cloudy night to stand on a high bluff and see the prarie on fire in all directions redening the clouds and rendering every limb, tree, and moving thing planely visable. I ran on ahead of the coach near half a mile to a high bluff where I counted twenty different fires. The one nearest to me was where the coach and horses were moving at a very slow pace up the bluff. The passengers were on foot and moved along behind and ahead of the coach in a direct line of fire. The glare from the burning prarie gave them an unearthly look which was wild and romantic in the extreme. I enjoyed it as but few can.

*Monday 30* — Daylight found us at a station awaiting breakfast. Passed as pleasant a night as I ever did in a Coach diversified with walks up and down the steepest hills. The wind changed this morning and seemed to threaten snow. I could easily discover we were getting farther North as the wind came down cold and raw from the North, where, within three hundred miles the snow lies three feet deep. About 8 o'clock we crossed the Nashnabotina[1] river in a Scow. The river had risen one foot during the night and was just ready to go out of its banks which will be worse than the Tarkeo and stop traviel. Here Commenced a slow driszeling cold rain which continued all day. The rain had the effect to hasten on our drivers so that our prospects were favorable of reaching Council Bluffs as early as eight o'clock.

At Sidney forty-five miles from Council Bluff we were relieved of six of our passengers, leaving but five in the Coach making the balance of our ride more comfortable. The first station we stoped at after leaving Sidney was at a farm house on the open prarie. Mr. Jackson, a Cincinnati man and Myself went in to warm. The lady of the house, a woman about fifty years of age, questioned us closely about affairs in Kansas. She knew something was going to be done as some of them *abolitionests* had been to the neighborhood and taken away the guns they left there last fall. I told her there would be no more trouble, all was quiet. She could not believe it. Eyed me very suspiciously, then asked how that hole came in my hat. My traveling companions took the hint at once and told the lady I was one of the Kansas prisoners who had escaped. I found it was useless for me to try to make a fair statement of affairs, and was obliged to own up and tell all about how we had been treated. I made every thing fare implicating no one. When we left our hostess seemed to be satisfied as she had seen the elephant.

The hole in the hat was on the brim. While on the upper deck on the steamer a spark droped on my hat and had burned a hole as round

---

[1] Nishnabotna.

and about the size of a rifle ball. This was what attracted the attention of the inquisitive lady.

At St Mary's our last change of horses and twelve miles from Council Bluffs we learned the Steamer Admiral which had left St. Josephs the day before we did, had not yet passed up. We were 24 hours behind time still ahead of the boat. At six o'clock we left St Marys expecting to be at the Bluffs as early as half past eight. The road ran along the bottoms and was in a bad state owing to the continued rain of the last twelve hours. Night had set in by the time we had made six miles. At this point was a sluce some twenty feet wide and about as deep. The watter was out of the banks and overflowed a large space on the bottoms both sides of the bridge. In the midst of the water before reaching the bridge the horses got set and could not move the coach. We were all obliged to get out and into the water three feet deep and wade to dry land. The water was cold as ice. Our boots were full and more was pattering down on our heads while a cold north wind sent its chilling blasts almost through us. We stood a few minutes in this condition while the driver tried to make his horses draw out the empty coach, but without success. What was to be done! No house was near, and to stand still was not deemed safe, in our wet and chilling condition. The driver wished us to wade in and unfasten his horses, while he remained on the Coach, thus enabling him to get on one of the horses and get away without *his* getting in the watter. We declined however as we think he might have went around another road and thus prevented this Catastrophe. Each Man waded back to the coach and got his carpet sack and flounced along throug the water to the bridge. Here we rested a few minutes and plunged in on the other side, and for near one hundred rods we waded knee deep and some of the way up to the seat of our pants. It was a trying time but the only alternative. The excitement kept the watter from chilling us through. Reaching the dry ground a ground as dry as could be during a rain we paddled on the best we could with our heavy Carpet Sacks boots filled with water, clothes wet and stif, and at every step our feet sticking like tar to the muddy prarie soil. We looked in vain for a farm house by the way. After a short walk we discovered a light across the prarie, glimmering faintly through the darkness of the night and the falling rain. One of our party said he thought it was at Council Bluffs, and if so it must be four miles. This information was rather discouraging. We consoled ourselves however with the belief that the light could not be over one and a half miles at the extent. We draged ourselves along for one whole hour until it seemed we could go no farther. Still that deceptive light receeded from us as fast as we traveled, and we could not discover that it was any nearer than when we started. I could easily imagine how one benight on the prarie in a snow storm would become disheartened and lay down and take his last sleep while the winter wind covered him with pure white sheet of snow. Another half hour and instead of one light we could discover some dozen or more. This animated us afresh at the same time we had another hundred *yards* to wade in mud and water above our knees. Our last half mile we paid no attention to the best part of the road so we made headway. At ten o'clock we reach the *Paciffic House* Council Bluffs. My head was dizzy and I could barely see while my arms seemed pulled down to the ground by my heavy satchel. We had walked six miles.

Two of our number on reaching Council Bluffs were by their own firesides surrounded by their own families. What a blessing there homes must have been that night. Three of us stoped at the hotel, ordered a room with a fire and two buckets of water. By assisting each other we succeeded in getting off our boots, which was a difficult job with what streangth we had left. As soon as I could arrange my clothes around the stove and wash the mud from my feet and legs, I *tumbled* into bed, not "careing whether School Kept or not."

*Tuesday 31* — Got up feeling much better than I could have expected, put on my pants which were about half dry, a clean pair of Sock and a pair of new boots which I bought at St. Louis, Stowing My muddy boots into My satchel. It had Seased raining but was cold and foggy, very much such a morning as the one I first saw here last fall. After breakfast took the omnibus and reached Omaha about 10 o'clock. To my great regret found Mr. Tuttle had gone east. He left a letter for me however which was some consolation. After spending half hour at the Bank where I met a number of the Saratoga men I went down to Mr. Rogers to see Br. Cook. I will not say we were glad to see each other. We were overjoyed. Cook felt bad when he learned I had Not caled to Flint.

He had rather have paid My extra expences than not to have me have gone there. Took dinner where Cook boards and decided to stop there until Sunday night. We must then both seek a new place. The *cheapest* board I can hear of is five dollars for day boarders and eight dollars where one lodges. The Family where Mr Cook boards consists of the man and wife with nine children the oldest is a Son Married whose wife also lives in the same family, they also have five day boarders and they only occupy *one* room, without a closet pantry or any out house and live up stairs. A curtain divides the room in the center one side is the dining room the other has a bed cook stove and all kitchen furniture. At night the beds are spread over the floor for the family and in the morning piled up in a corner. Such is Cook's boarding house without the least exageration.

After dinner called on my old acquaintance. At the Bank Met Dr. Kellum Brother of the young man I saw at Auban and later at Leavenworth as I came up. Dr Kellem's is the place I called one evening with Mr & Mrs Tuttle last fall. They were then building a brick house over their heads. I accepted an invitation to tea very gladly. Was much pleased with Mrs Kellum and her daughter one year younger than Sophia. They live in eastern style and comfortable. They had invited *another* one of the *dignitary* to supper who had lately arrived. It was Gov. Richardson of Mich. We had a pleasant time and a good supper after which I returned to the store where I occupied the bunk of one of the workmen who was out on the prarie proveing up his claim. Slept good all Night.

*Wednesday, April 1.* — Feel the worse for wear, the excitement Kept me up yesterday, today I am lame and sore, and feel the effects of my Journey, particularly the last Six Miles, spent most of the day dozing over the stove in Cooks workshop trying to get rested. Met Mr. Warner to day.

*Thursday 2.* — Not fully rested. Walked about the town and up on the bluffs with Mr. Warner. Business has not yet fully commenced here for the want of lumber from up the river which is daily expected.

This afternoon spent a season with Secretary Brown and others of the Saratoga Co. Was posted up on their future proceedings. A hotel to be called the *Trinity House* and commenced last fall is to be completed by the first of June. This belongs to the Saratoga Company and is paid for. A Hotel Company has been organised to put up a Most Magnificent hotel comprising an entire block and to cost $100,000. The plans were got up in Philadelphia. The contract for the stone work and foundation is let and will be commenced in a few days. The hotel is to be Completed in one year. There is to be 200 buildings put up in Saratoga this summer. Most of them are under Contract and only waiting for lumber to commence. I reported Myself ready to take hold Next Monday. I am to make out a scedule for the drawing of the lots. There is to be 15 lots to each Share drawn on the 17th. I have become Somewhat animated today which has driven away the blues.

*Friday 3d.* — A pleasant and warm day. Walked up to the "Trinity House" and over part of the Saratoga Town plot. The more I see of it the better I like it. It is *delightful! charming!!* and by far a pleasanter location than Omaha. The Company donate 256 lots to churches schools and individuals who will build before July first. I am in for one. Have completely recovered from my fatigue of the journey.

*Saturday Evening 4th.* — I have been to tea and am seated in Cooks work shop where I have spent every evening since I arrived in this place. This is the night of all others when my mind flies back to my own fireside. In immagination I see you all seated around a warm fire in a comfortable room. Irwin and Sophia wondring where father is tonight. They may sing with truth, "My father's on the wild prarie," for it is a wild night, not cold but the wind blows a hurricane and shakes this frail cottonwood building, creeping in to every crevice rattling my paper as I write. How I wish I could form one of the groop this evening. That cannot be so I will banish the Thought.

The day has been a windy one. Have Kept in doors most of the time. Talked a good deal about Saratoga projects. It is the theme now. What I shall make out of it is yet to be ascertained. I am not sorry yet that I have come out here. What another week will bring forth we cannot tell except we will have one the less to live.

One thing I forgot to Mention in its proper place. When I left home I had between ninety and one hundred dollars. I arrived here the 31st ult with but nine dollars, and my trunk to be paid for bringing from St. Josephs to this point. I believe I can travel as economicus as any one but this trip has taken the money off fast. I hope it will come back as rapidly and more easy.

We learn by Mail to day of the appointment of a Robert J. Walker of Mississipi Governor of Kansas. I fear it will cause more trouble. My 40th page is full. I will bid you good night. E. F. BEADLE

Omaha City April 5, 1857
Dear Wife and Children

It is Sunday and a very cold one. The wind has been blowing from the north since yesterday morning, and today we can only Keep Comfortable by getting close to the hot Stove. I shall not venture out to church today.

Tomorrow morning will be four weeks since I left home. Fifteen hundred miles over mountains, praries, rivers and Lakes intervenes between us, seperating as as widely as would the ocean. The weeks will undoubtedly be lengthened into as many months before we meet again. This is truly an unnatural way for a man of a family to live, but deeming it for the best we must try and be content. Letter writing is the only means by which we can communicate with each other. As yet I have not heard a word direct from home and expect it will be another week still before I get a letter. After that I hope to receive one every week. Cook gets one regular as the weeks come and I think where there is two or three to write you can write as often as Elizabeth does. You must bear in mind that a letter from ones home when far away, is much more welcome than a letter *can* be from the absent one, when you are surrounded by warm friends and relatives and all the comforts of life.

I left orders at the Barnum House St. Louis to have any letters that should come for me to be forwarded to this place.

You have, enclosed, the balance of my diary up to the date of this. I shall continue it for the present at least and mail once a

week. Until the roads get more settled I shall send my letters by
the boats to St Louis as it now takes ten days for the mails to cross
the state by Coach.

It is impossible for me to form any correct estimate of what
My prospects will be here this Summer. I shall know better when
Mr. Tuttle returns from the east. I think however that I shall do
well judging from present prospects. Mr. Brown was over anxious
for me to go to Lawrence with him. Offered me one thousand
per year and if that was not enough he would give me twelve
hundred. I could not accept even if I desired it.

Rents here are enormously high, houses of one room fifteen
feet square rent at $25. per month. Provisions are in the same
proportion. Wood $6 per cord. Dry goods and apples are quite
reasonable the latter are as cheap as in the city of New York $6.
per barrell. Unless more farmers Come in provisions will keep up
for a number of years yet. I do not deem it advisable to think of
moving my family to this place until buildings are more pleanty.
Many famlies live in houses no larger or better than our wood
house. Such a house as we live in at Cold Springs before we built
would rent for $30. per month. This would seem discouraging
to emigration but wages are in proportion. I believe if there was
five hundred dwellings now ready for tenants they would be filled
by the first of June. When I left St. Josephs there were some fifty
families awaiting a boat for this place. When they come I know
not what they will do as there is not a vacant house in town and
the hotels are full. Boats are daily expected with lumber which
will be speedily put into dwellings.

I hope and trust you are comfortable so far as the necessities of
life go. Necessities in Buffalo are luxuries in Omaha. I wish Some
one would buy the house in Buffalo as I cannot say how I shall
be prepared to meet the payments. As it respects your going East
this summer you must do as you think best. But try and keep the
children to school for should they come to this place they will
not have the advantages they do at Buffalo.

*Irwin* How do you get along with your school and doing the
work of splitting wood, and going of errends now father is away.

I presume your are the best boy now you ever was. I have been looking at a Mustang Pony which I think some of buying for you in you Come out here this fall. Then you can take Sophia out a riding on the prarie in a little buggy or go a horse back ride with her. You be a good boy and get your lessons well and when you come to Omaha you shall have a horse.

*Sophia* I have not received one of those letters you were going to write me. I presume however you have written but the letters have not arrived. I shall look for a letter every week after they commence coming. I wish you could step in and see what a bed and room pa has to sleep in. I am to have a new boarding place tomorrow where I shall lodge and perhaps faar better. You must be good and kind to your mother brothers and aunt Sarah and learn fast at school and how to do housework at home, for when you come to Omaha you and Mother will have to do all the work. Give my Love to Aunt Sarah and Charlott.

*Mate* Cook says he shall not move his family here unless I do, as there is no womans help to be had and should Lib be sick she must suffer. When help can be got it is one dollar per day. Washing is ten cents a piece. When one comes both must. You can then help each other. One of the boys in the family where I board does the washing. There is Eight boys and one girl in the family.

My health is usually good. The first night on the steamboat on the Mo. I took cold since which time I have been troubled with a cough. Nothing alarming however although unpleasant. I think it is getting better.

I think I have written enough for this time. Kiss the children for me and remember me to My friends and relatives.

*Affectionately*
*E. F. Beadle.*

*Monday 6.* — The wind went down with the sun last Night but it had blowed from the north long enough to bring down the arctic region weather and water in our basin two inches deep froze solid. This is Omaha the 6th of April.

The River continueing to rise prevents communication from the
Iowa side and we have no mails from the East today. My cold has
settled on my lungs. My chest is very sore and I have a severe pain in
my back between my shoulders. If I was home I should be down sick.

In looking up a new boarding place I have been very fortunate,
through the intersessions of Mr. Warner, in getting in at Mr. Estabrook's
the Attorney General of the territory. I could not have got a better place
in the territory. They have no boarders except Mr Warner and myself.
The Family consists of Mrs Estabrook's Father and three other Male
relatives of the family two children a girl Eleven and a boy two years of
age. Mr Estabrook is in Wisconsin on business. The three male relatives
are going out on their claim in a few days when I shall have a chance to
sleep at the house where I can doctor up. Mr. E has horses Cows and
poltry and we live first rate "*real human.*" Augusta Estabrook is a very
good substitut for Sophia as she is a Singer and plays on the guitar.

The wind has changed to the south and the weather is fast moderating
and tonight Spring again.

*Tuesday 7.* — The Big Muddy is Mad and gone out of its banks, has
not been so high in twenty years. It is said that teams cannot cross on
account of the bottoms being overflowed between Sioux City Iowa and
St Joseph Mo a distance by the river of 500 miles. We can get no mails
from the east. This morning was very mild. At breakfast Augusta was
trying to get some of the men to go for a horseback ride with her, but
they were going away on business and I offered to go. The Pony was got
out and one of the horses but the rain setting in prevented. Went to the
shop and up to Florence, Six miles, in a covered buggy with Mr. Cook
to contract for coal. I thought I would try going out. But it rained all
the way and the wind blew strong from the north west, so that when I
got back my cold was not much better. Took some medicine at noon.
Spent the afternoon with Saratoga Co. After tea the baby danced while
the little girl played on the guitar and the grandfather on the violin.
The apples were then passed around after which I came up to the shop
and wrote the above. The boarding place I now have makes me forget I
am on the borders of sivilization. My back pains me dreadfully tonight.

*Wednesday 8.* — It is evening, the weather has moderated, and it is delightful out of doors after such a cold wind as we have had. The Moon is in its full and the river bottoms which are not overflowed are dotted with prarie fires. Many people are out enjoying the evening. Notwithstanding the winds here, we have weather that cannot be approached by New York where I have lived. I am becoming More and More attached to the place and trust it will be my future home, and If I had a house I should wish my family was here today.

Feel the most like myself today of any day since I have been here. My lameness has mostly left me. The cough however still hangs on. We have had three mails from the east since last night, they were brought over in a skiff. I got no letters. Cook did. I have been working with Mr Warner a little to day helping him build a fence around one of his lots. He is to help me in return. The River is Still rising.

Mrs. Estabrook gave me some interesting details of her pioneer life when they first came to the Territory. They lived in what they now use as a barn, (it is not fit for horses) it is very low, and at the time the family occupied it, its only roof was made by puting a few small polls lengthwise and covering them with prarie grass, had no boards on the floor but covered the ground with hay and spread down a rag carpet and put in such furniture as they could procure, the house being on descending ground when it rained the water would run through the hay under the carpet and pass out on the other side. One night during a thunder storm a hole broke through the hay rooffing, the rain poard in faster than it would run out and they were forsed to use a wash tub most of the night, carrying it out as often as it filled which was every few minutes. This was the way our Attourny general lived when he first came here. How would Mrs. Beadle like this mode of living.

*Thursday 9.* — A pleasant morning. Took a horseback ride immediately after breakfast. Little Augusta Manages her pony like a skillful rider as she is. She is the smallest girl I ever saw ride a horseback. She will dash up bluffs and down ravines and over prarie as fast as I have wished to ride, and I am not sure but she would be a better guardian for me than I for her. When she was but three years old her father would ride out

with her tying her to her horse so she would not fall and then gallop
off at full speed. She will lend her pony to my pet as she calls Sophia.

Worked on the fence with Mr Warner part of the day and devoted
some time to the Saratoga enterprise. The river continues to rise. No
boat up. I got a paper this afternoon from some one in Buffalo. The
paper was the daily Republic of March 16th. On the wrapper was
(Kirby). I can not think who sent it as I can call to mind no one
of my acquaintance by that name. Whoever he may be I hold myself
under obligations to him. The paper looked like an old friend, and I
read it adv. and all. I miss a daily after tea very much. We shall soon
have one here a Mr Wyman our present P. M. has gone east for the type
and press.

My lameness and cold has settled in the glands of my throat since
morning and I can hardly swallow. I shall doctor up tonight, as I
commence to lodge at my boarding house. Mr. Warner was just as
I am soon after he came here.

There is a meeting of land agents called this evening to fix a tarrif of
prices. If my throat is not too bad I shall surely attend.

*Friday, 10.*   Attended the meeting last evening. We organized a Stock
board. Became acquainted with many new business men, and have
spent the most of this day talking up the business of last evening and
arranging for a permanent organization for our individual benifit and
the benifit of eastern Capitalist who are becoming imposed upon by
false representations.

The Pawnee Indians are camped near here. The old men women
and children. The strong and healthy are out on a Buffalo hunt. Those
remaining here hang about the houses begging their living, stealing cats,
dogs, and the refuse of the slaughter houses. Some one trying what he
could do with his revolver shot a fine dog about a week ago. Today
the indians found it, and although it had commenced putrifying, they
squat down skined it and carried it off to cook. Such is about the best
food the filthy Pawnees get while the hunters are away.

River still rising. Weather mild and pleasant this evening. My throat
is well, and the only lameness I have is probably occasioned by my not
being used to horse back riding, and the horse I had was a hard rider.

Owing to the rise in the river and prevailing north Winds no boats have got up yet. The river rising makes the current more rapid.

*Saturday 11.* A cold north wind blowing again. A Man from Fremont a town west of the Elkhorn came here for provisions and in crossing the Elkhorn on his return which was on a rise, was drowned. The Elkhorn and Platt are both impossible at this time, with wagons.

*Great Excitement on the frontier! Attack upon the settlers by the Pawnees!! A Pawnee shot!!!* — Mr. John Davis, Justice of the peace at Salt creek Lancaster Co. N. T. arrived here this Morning about 10 o'clock calling upon The Governor for Melitia to assist in exterminating the Pawnees. Mr. Davis reports that depridations have been frequent during this fall, winter and present Spring, untill they have lost their oxen horses cattle and in fact every thing the Indians could drive or run off. On Tuesday a number of Pawnees came to Salt creek, painted and in war costume, demanding the lands and pay for the deer and woolves the whites had killed or they would kill and scalp them, that they had taken the fort and scalped the people, that there was a party of one hundred and fifty Pawnees in the rear which would soon be up. The present party continued in the vicinity all night hooting and yelping. About daylight they approached the house of Mr. Davis with threatening signs, one of the Pawnees raised his gun apparently in the act of shooting — but was not quick enough as a ball from Mr. Davis gun killed him on the spot. The balance fled. Mr Davis fearing a further attack burried the dead Indian and started with his family towards Plattsmouth which is on the same side of the Platt River at Salt Creek. Before reaching Plattsmouth, he was met by a party of six men and their families going to Salt Creek. Mr. Davis give up his gun to them and left his wife in their charge, himself continuing on to Plattsmout where he was taken across the Platt in a skiff. At Bellview he got a man to bring him here. He had in his company another aggrevved individual who had been a great looser by the Pawnees.

The Governor did not feel like calling on the Malitia and rushing upon the Pawnees until he knew more of the affair. He however despatched General Thayer to the vicinity of Salt creek, with orders if necessary to call on the Militia of that Lancaster County. This was not wholly satisfactory to Mr Davis who wanted to raise a company of volinteers and exterminate the whole race of Pawnees. In this he had the sympathy of a cerntain officer of *this* Territory who has just resigned at Washington with a view of being elected to Congress. His object is probably to get the Squatters vote. The said official resides at Bellview and took Mr Davis and friend in his Carriage to Bellview ready to head a party of volunteers.

The Governor said he did not believe an indian could be found in fifty miles of Salt Creek when they got there, but they probably would be revenged some day on Mr Davis. The Gov. further said the Indian agent was expected every hour and would go out at once and if he found it necessary he was the proper person to call on him, the Governor, and then the U. S. Government would pay the expences. I had an invetation to go with General Thayer, but the ex Indian agent wished to go and I was obliged to give way. I had got all ready as Gen Thayer was very anxious to have me go along. The Gen is I understand, another candidate for the same office as the other gentleman.

This afternoon I received a letter from Mr. McKim under date of March 26th. *Seventeen days* after I left Buffalo, still I get none from my own family. Did they wait *seventeen days* and not write to me? I am becoming very anxious about a letter from home. Could I get one tonight it would have been a great consolation as it is Saturday night when I think most of being home.

*Sunday 12* — The Steamer *Silver heels* came in during last night, bringing about 250 passenges. What is to be done with them I cannot tell. The boat brought no lumber or houses could be built in quick time. Mrs. Smith, the lady whose husband was left at Jef. City and who we left at Leavenworth over two weeks ago came up on the Silver heels, Mrs. Estabrook took them in giving them breakfast and dinner by that time they found two rooms for rent for $25. per Month. They have gone into them to make the best of it possible. Every family here has to be as accommodating as possible or the people would suffer. I cannot conceive where they all find shelter in Kansas. Troubles are anticepated in Kansas.

Through the Kindness of Mr. Smith who saw my trunk at the storehouse in St. Josephs. I received it by this boat. I have been aranging the contents. One of the new shirts I brought with me has been returned from the washer womans with a spot of iron rust on the bosom as large as the bowl of a tablespoon, quite an ornament.

This afternoon the wind is blowing again the way you never saw it blow down Niagara St.

I have an opportunity to send this by a Daughter of Mr Goodwills who is going to Batavia to Spend the Summer at school, or By a Col. Parker of the city of N. york. Shall go up and if not to late it will go by St Louis on the boat otherwise I will mail it.

The water in the river is between 16 and 17 feet above low water mark, between the Steamboat landing and the town there is a space 500 feet wide where in this strip of water the passengers must be taken across in a skiff. At Saratoga the landing is dry. The Steamer is to return tonight if the wind is not to high. Am about well again.

Again Good by

E. F. Beadle


*Monday, 13*  Watter going down in the river faster than it came up. Cold north winds continue but not blowing a gale. After dinner went up to Saratoga to show the gift lots to some strangers who wish to build. While on the platteau and revolving in my mind what would be the best part of the town I conceived a project, I believe will put money in my purse.

Returning to Omaha I learned a large eastern mail had been received, and went direct to the Post office. Found nothing in my box. Went to Cook's and there I found.

*A Letter from Home* — Yes a letter from my own fireside. No one can fully estimate the value of such a letter unless they have been in a like situation. Five weeks and a day had passed during which time we have travailed by all possible modes of conveyance night and day, been in eight different states and two territories. Mingled with all sorts of people from the frozen North to the Sunny South, until the distance that seperated me from my family seemed almost like that around the globe. At last however, after a tedious Journy over land, across river, lakes, streams, prarie and mountains my revered *Uncle "Sam"* opened his mail bags and dealt out to me a little parcel, which though very small bore an impress of home and produced a powerful effect like the doses dealt out by the hoemaopothists. A mingled sensation of joy and fear possessed me, were they all well if not well were they all living, had disease or death been there? There had been time for sad changes.

I took the letter unopened and went down to my boarding house. Mrs. Estabrook knew I had a letter as soon as she saw me. Threw down the letter on the table. Went down in the basement. Washed my face and hands and brushed my clothes, then went up into the sitting room and carefully opened the letter. There was a letter enclosed from each one. Those little fingers of my children had been busy in adding to the joy of there father who was far away. Now which one shall I read first. Cant read them all at a time, so I decided to take them in the order of the ages of the writers. I read each one a number of times which answered for my supper that night. My mind was so full of the thoughts brought up by the receipt of the letter I slept but little althoug all were well at home.

*Tuesday, 14.* — A steamer came in last evening. She is from Pittsburgh Pa. loaded with merchandize and furnature mostly the latter among which is some very nice better than has been in market heretofore. The boat is the Spread Eagle twenty-five days from Pittsburgh. She had on 40,000 feet dressed lumber for this place. Was told at some port below they could do better to sell it there which they did very much to their loss and our regret.

Figuring some on my new project. It will work well. A Company of forty came in this morning from across Iowa. Going to locate in Saratoga and work at gardening this summer. That will pay.

They have commenced to break ground today for a new hotel here to be called the Park house. The citizens have voted to sell their park to complete the Capitol building which was not appropriated for by the last Congress. Saratoga agrees to pay one fourth necessary to complete it. The building will be completed this summer at all events by the City itself.

*Wednesday 15* — Staked out a building lot in Saratoga, and selected a lot of shade trees and wild goosbury bushes on the bluff of the table land to set out in my lot as soon as it is fenced.

The Steamer "White Cloud" arrived here about seven o'clock this evening with 150 passengers and a good supply of provisions. Shingles, doors, and window sash, but no lumber as yet. Among the passengers I found two old acquaintances, one I traveled with last fall the other was the gentleman of whom I bought the large map we have of "our Country." His brother is the baptist minester of this place.

When the boat arrived it seemed onehalf of the inhabitants were at the landing. When the plank was put out they rushed on in such a body it was some minutes before the passengers could get off. Then such a peeping into each others faces to recognise some expected friend. The vicinity of the ladies cabin was one perfect jam of men eagerly peeping over the heads of more forward ones or crowding through to get a sight at some dozen ladies who were as eager to single out, their husband, brother, or friend. I mixed in but no one I knew was there. I was not however as disappointed as some hundred others must have been.

Not as windy today or as cold but it froze hard last night. It has been cold over a week. We hope for a change.

*Thursday 16* A delightful day and no wind. Have spent the day in showing up strangers. Been up to Saratoga. Every on goes off in ecstases about the location. Can sell lots as soon as they are divided. The Steamer Emigrant came in about five this afternoon. About seventy-five passengers and a supply of lumber.

Clouded up at dark to rain as it was warm but the rain came down in Snow. Went up to the Post office at eight o'clock. The ground was white with snow but warm air. Got a letter from Brother Frank. Went to bed as tired as I want to be. Had the nightmare and was nearvous all night. This was an awful one to Me.

*Friday 17* — Two inches of snow this morning, with a prospect of clearing off. Prospects however have deceived us and it has snowed steadily all day, driving from the Northeast. There is probably a foot of snow on a level, and still it is coming down as fast as ever. I never recollect but one such time. That was at Cooperstown many years ago. The snow then fell three feet. The storm does not discourage me with making Nebraska my home. "Where there is a will there is a way." I also understand this cold weather we have had has prevailed south and east.

The Steamer "Minnehaha" came in this afternoon with another hundred passengers and more lumber. We are now having a boat daily. Where the passengers all get a chance to stand up, even, under cover, I cannot conceive, I ventured up town this afternoon and could see two or three to each door asking for board. I cannot too much appritiate my boarding place. — Good Night.

*Saturday, 18 of April 1857* — This is a most delightful January morning. The Sun shines clear and bright and the snow sparcles and crisps under foot like mid winter. Last evening about dark Cook came down and told me General Thayer wished to see me about going to Plattsmouth with him. The General had been notified of further outrages by the Pawnees. Some whites were out looking for the stock they had left previous when they were attacked by the Pawnees, with whom they had a brush. One white man and two indians were killed and three indians taken prisoners. The whites then retreated to *Weaping Water* where there is a few squatters cabins. Here at last accounts they were surrounded by the Pawnees.

Not finding the General at his house or office I went down to the Minnehaha where he had engaged passage and awaited his arrival. We then put on board five boxes of U. S. Muskets one Sixpounder and a supply of ammunition. The General was to take no one with him but wished me to go along (by the way Mr Brown introduced me here as Doctor Beadle. I am accordingly called Dr by most of the people). The Dr. agreed to go. The boat was to leave this morning at daylight. Gen. Thayer was to be on board the boat at daylight. I thought of going on the same evening, but getting somewhat wet being out so long in the snow and my throat sore I took some ginger tea and doctored up to take an early start. This morning got up at daylight but could not see the boat so I went back to bed disappointed. When I got up an hour after the boat was just leaving. I felt crest-fallen. My ambition for glory fell below Zero. I anticepated great sport in organizing a company at plattsmouth and going out to Weaping Water. Not that I expectd we should be called upon to fire again, for in this case I should prefer to be away, particular when there was no one to engage with but the poor miserable Pawnees. There would have been however a novelty in the enterprize and perhaps I might have been *promoted*.

Claim jumpers are being brought up daily. Most of them forego their claimed right on the decision of the Club who give them a fair and impartial trial. Occasionally however one is found who is stuborn and will not at once yeald. One of this class was tried last evening and this morning but would not abide by the decision of the club which was for him to yield his claim and withdraw his filling. The captain of "the regulators" is our Mayor a man six and a half feet high and well proportioned. He took the claim jumper by the collar escorted him down into the street, and with a dozen or fifteen men with loaded muskets they started for the "big Muddy." In general the prisoner comes to terms. What was the result in this case I cannot say. The party returned without the prisoner and no questions asked. There is no law here except club laws and vigilance committee to enforce them. A man gets a fair hearing and justice done him but it is quick done and no heavy expence saddled on the County. I am not sure but in most cases this is the best plan. All are agreed and a man knows what to depend upon. I think I will be quiet and peacible.

No mail east of Iowa today. Mr Warner Mrs. Estabrook and myself were expecting letters. We were however all alike disappointed and could sympathise with each other. Mrs. Estabrooks disappointment resulted in the return of her husband which she was not expecting for one or two weeks. Mr E reported the roads in a fine state across Iowa. Which makes Mr Warner and Myself wonder the more that we do not get more letters.

This day has been as warm a one as any we have had since I have been here this Spring and has melted the snow rapidly. The Steamer "Florence" came in this evening discharged her freight for this place and passed up to Florence.

*Sunday 19* — Soon after breakfast the Steamer "Omaha" came in bound for 'Sioux City. Mr. Estabrook and Myself went down to the boat which was loaded as full as she could hold. Among the freight which has been discharged within the past few days we found large quantities of provisions, Lumber and fruit trees. Business will now fairly commence and in one year the yards will be ornamented with shrubbery and fruit trees giving every thing an Eastern air.

This has been a delightful day and one half of the ground is bare again. I begin to be uneasy for some regular business. The drawing of the lots in Saratoga which was to have taken place the 17th has been adjourned two weeks awaiting the return of Mr Tuttle. A meeting of the board is to be held Wednesday the 22d when I am to submit a written proposition to them for their action. I do so at their request. I cannot say whether it will be accepted or not. If it is it will be money in the pockets of Saratoga owners, and I believe a small pile in my own.

The claim jumper that was taken off yesterday held out until they threw him into the river three times. They attached a rope to him threw him into the "big Muddy" then pulled him out if he was not then ready to forego his claim they would Souse him in again, repeating the dose until he came to terms, which was not until he had been in the third time.

The Steamer Florence stoped at Saratoga, discharged some freight and one passenger. This is the first boat that ever stoped at Saratoga and Dr. J. Seymor the first passenger ever landed. The freight was some brick machines and six carriages for Wm. Young Brown. This is the commencement of commercial business in Saratoga. E. F. BEADLE

*Monday 20, April 1856* — A raw disagreeable day. Remained in doors speculating on the contents of a letter which I expected at twelve noon. Did not get the letter. Felt a little out of sorts. Mr Estabrook suggested that I hint to my wife that divorces are very easily obtained in this country and perhaps she would be more prompt. Fearing she would not write at all if I should, I refrain from mentioning the matter at all.

*Tuesday, 21* — Assisted Mr Estabrook this forenoon in copying some legal papers. The snow has disappeared. The Steamer "Col. Crossman" arrived and departed today.

*Wednesday, 22* — Presented my proposition, in writing, to the Sulphur Spring Land Co. Took a stroll down at the South part of Omaha among the hazle brush and prarie cane. Passed thru occupied Pawnee tents. Two Pawnee boys came out half naked and wanted I should give them five cents to shoot at a mark. On the side of a bank I found where a mud hut of the Pawnees had been during the winter. The ground in the vicinity was strewed with bones of animals of various size including skulls of cats, dogs, deers, horses and cattle. The vicinity resembled the entrance to a wolfs den more than that of a human habitation.

I sat down by the side of a lake formed by the high water of the Missouri, and remained motionless for a half hour. The wild ducks came up within ten feet of me and fed along the bank. There were some beautiful ones. If I had had a good shot gun I could have killed a fine lot of them. Or even with my revolver had it been with me I could have killed some they came so close to me.

*Thursday, 23* — Two Steamers came in this morning at daylight, "The Edinburg" and "Admiral." I went down before breakfast. Both boats were well loaded with passengers and lumber. The latter is very much wanted here as the little that has come has been mostly used even at $100. per thousand which is the price asked for lumber at this time. The same lumber can be bought in Buffalo at $16 per thousand.

Having written this much immediately after breakfast I was called upon by a carpenter from Centralia Ill. whom I induced while there to come here. He has two other carpenters and his brother with him. They have brought their household furnature and are going to select a gift Lot in Saratoga pitch their tent and go to work. Imediately after dinner I shall go up with them to select their lot.

They brought a present for me from Harriet. It was a small paper box about eight or ten inches square in which was a fruit cake a piece of sponge cake a lemon and some nuts, with a line requesting me to dived with Cook. You see I am remembered by some one.

Today's mail brings me a letter from Mr. Adams, from which I learn all are well at home. I would like the information to come from home itself. The letter was dated April 10th. It contained intelligence of the final result of Thomas & Lathrops failure. Notwithstanding all they done towards, I feel sorry for them. Misery you know loves company. I am glad to learn that Irwin and Frank are in Auburn.

The weather has become pleasant and business is on the move and our town filled with Strangers. Cooperstown is well represented. One store here has four clerks from C. Two of the number is J. Collins and Parley Johnson. During the arrivals of the last week Joseph McNeal and Wm. Pitcher came to town to work at gardening, Mr Tuttle sent them on.

*Evening.*  Went up immediately after dinner with My Centralia friends and staked out a lot in Saratoga. They at once despatched a team for their effect. They had two waggon loads, they were to arrange their boxes in the form of a hollow square. Put up their stove. Cook their first meal in the territory, and sleep the first night under their tent. Tomorrow they will have up a temporary cabin covered with cloth. This is the correct way to do instead of paying six dollars per week for board and they will fare about as well as to board. Their Company consists of four. One person is only fourteen years of age and he is to be their Cook. The weather is fine and they will have great times. They have a violin and base viol with them to make evening music. I have an invitation to dine with them on wild duck as soon as they shoot one. Their location is lot ten in block 266 near the Trinity house which I find is beginning to look up some. I noticed seven commencements of new buildings since I was last up to Saratoga. What a change there will be in the next two months.

Returning to Mr. Estabrooks at 5 o'clock I found the horses ready for my second horseback ride with Augusta and we had a pleasant ride for an hour before tea.

While I am writing in my room Mr. Estabrook and his family are in the sitting room making fine music. Mr. E. is playing the violin and singing base. Mrs E. and the little girl are singing other parts and they fill the house with music.

This day I go into the streets where I am at home and acquainted and I feel like a stranger there are so many strange faces here, and this evening the streets are filled with the *elite* of Omaha. I could not believe there was so many moving bundles of dry goods in town. The silks and satins are fluttering on Farnnham Street equal to our No! Your Main st. Buffalo ain't no where when Compared to Omaha or Saratoga. We are a fast people here, last fall when I was here there was not a piano in town, now there is over a dozen.

There has been a few Omaha Indians in town today. They are splendid looking fellows, finely and gaudily dressed in all the trappings of the proudest red men. I would attempt a description but have not time to night as it is bed time. Will do so hereafter. The Omahas are a great contrast to the filthy Pawnees who go half naked. I could look a half day on the noble Omahas.

*Friday noon 24th* — Took a horse back ride up to Saratoga to give directions about buildings, found my friends had got a load of lumber and commenced their house. Had a fine time the past night, had a carpet spread on the prarie and every thing comfortable. The cabin formed by boxes was not high enough to stand up in. The stove was outside. Continued my ride up to Florence.

*Saturday 25 — Another Sad Chapter in My diary.* Among the passengers that came up the river when I did was a Mr Baker his wife son and daughter from Western New York. Mr Bakar came here in the winter and made arrangements to establish a nursery got 300,000 trees and grafts at Rochester and started early with his family for Omaha. His son was eleven years of age and his daughter seven. The little girl on the boat was taken down with the Whooping Cough and the first day was quite sick with a high fever. After that was well except her Cough which was severe. At St. Joseph Mr Bakers family was among the number that were obliged to wait for another boat to go up to Omaha. They came up on the steamer "Silver heels" on Sunday the 12 the same time Mr and Mrs Smith, which I have written about, came up. The little girl was around the cabin but one Eye was red as blood from Coughing which had strained her Eyes very much. The boy had been taken with the hay fever and was confined to his bed. They were acquaintance of Mr Goodwill of this place, who took them in charge. From time to time I learned both the children were quite sick. Yesterday I had started to go up to Saratoga in the afternoon. Was met by Mr Goodwill who told me both the children were dead and it was then time for the funeral. The girl had died at noon and the boy at evening of the day previous. I attended the funeral, and you may readily imagine it was a heartrending scene. The only children of the family a boy and girl lay side by side in their . . . seperate coffins. The little girl had on, in her coffin, a string of coral beads to which was attached a little lockett. You cannot conceive the feelings the sight gave me. The balance of the afternoon was a gloomy one to me. Oh how homesick I was.

There was a large funeral and all seemed to sympathise with the afflicted parents. Such is the incidents of life and we must submit, heartrending as they are to us.

Having written this much since breakfast and mended Miss Augusta's doll for her company today I will leave my writing and walk up to Saratoga on business.

At Saratoga we found our Carpenters had got their frame up and a canvass over it and were writing for their families. Mr. Warner and myself selected our gift lots and intended commencing our improvements soon and when we are obliged to leave our present boarding house we shall keep house by ourselves. We may have to leave when Mrs E commences house cleaning as she thinks of visiting her friends in Wisconsin this summer. As long as they keep any one Mr Warner and myself can stay.

The traveling has so much improved across the State of Iowa Mr. Cook got his letter today which he usually gets on Mondays. I have been *seven weeks* away and got *one* letter. I *was* to have one *every week* when I left. Think not because *I write* every day and you know every act of mine of interest, and know that I am *well*, that I have *no* interest in hearing *occasionally* from *home*. I will however stop my complainings and say no more about your *not* writing, act your own pleasure. And at the same time remember I am not where I can pass my time as pleasantly as among relatives and friends. But on the borders of Civilization with but little to relieve the monotony of pionier life.

*Sunday 26* — We have a cold raw wind from the north making it unpleasant out of doors and I have been content to remain within today, reading "the hills of the Shatemuc."

The first bell in nebraska was hung yesterday on the Methodist church and to day we have "The sound of a churchgoing bell." It is a small affair and sounds like the Market bell of Buffalo, but will answer for Omaha. We shall have one worth hearing on the Presbyterian church we are to build in Saratoga this Summer. Br. Cook called down this evening and spent an hour or two.

*Monday 27* — Nothing of importance today other than the acceptance of my proposition by the Saratoga Company. Went up and staked out my lot. A delightful day.

*Tuesday 28* — Spent the day in the Saratoga Enterprise. Have partially agreed to put up a warehouse in Saratoga. The Steamer St. Mary's is up today. Received a letter from Cousin Benjamin of Memphis. The family were greatly disappointed at not seeing me there as I wrote them. Some of the family waited home two weeks for me. We have had a summer day this. We have no springs here. It steps at once from winter to summer.

*Wednesday, 29* — Took Mr. Estabrook's horse and buggy and rode down some six or eight miles to a sawmill where there was oak timber and ordered some fence posts saw'd for my Saratoga lots where I am to put up a cabin. The buggy ride was over a most delightful country having a variety of prarie and timber land. I went alone and had all pleasure to myself. Some of the farmers on the route are living in a hole in the ground for want of time to build better dwellings. The farmers are destined to become wealthy if they half work as their land will yield the greatest abundance and they have a market almost at their own door. What a wonderful change has taken place on this side of the river in three years.

Got home from the Mill to a late dinner, spent the afternoon in figuring.

*Thursday, 30* — Have passed a very unpleasant night. Soon after going to bed last evening, I went to sleep and awoke again in an hour after. I had dreamed I was, as I am, far away from home. Intelligence reached me of the death and burial of Sophia. My mind was so troubled it was a long while before I could get to sleep again, and when I did sleep my dreams were the same. My Brother Frank came to tell me what I had before heard of, Sophias death. Then one after another came my relatives to sympathize with me. At last came Mate who like the others told me the circumstances and expressed much sympathy. All however looked upon as the only mourner.

I awoke as many as a dozen times during the night but as soon as I got to sleep again the dreams haunted me and so great was my grief I would awake again but could not keep awake. There is a great deal of scarlet fever here and there has a number of children died with it. We were talking of it yesterday afternoon. I suppose that is one cause of dreaming as I did. My mind is this morning in Buffalo.

The Steamer "E. H. Gordon" is up from St. Louis. I am now going down to see what is on board.

Found the "Gordon" well loaded with grain and lumber. Also brought up some one hundred Danes bound for Salt Lake to Join the Mormons.

Between eight and nine o'clock a slow drizzelling rain from the north east set in, and we have had a north easter all day. The rain is just what is wanted here. I only went out when the Great Eastern mail came in. And I got at the Post office — What do you think? A letter! No! fifty cents worth of postage stamps and the Herald of Freedom from Mr Brown. A gloomy lonesom day.

*Friday May 1, 1857* — The storm which was raging last night at bed time, spent its fury before morning and the sun rose clear with a fair prospect of one of the finest days of the season. After breakfast went up to the office to Mail some papers and found four numbers of *The Home* for Mr. Hall who works for Cook. I never saw The Home look so well. Its familiar face wore a happy smile. It seems better printered and on better paper than it used to be. I presume that is occasioned by the distance it is from the office where it eminates, as printing offices are never the neatest places in the world. I feel a stronger attachment for "The Home" than I ever did before. The articles seem improved and the magazine generally wears an air of prosperity. I hope it will be sufficiently remunerative to warrant its continuance by its present publishers. It is one of the best publications, if not *the very best* in the country, and it must and will continue to be appreciated and its circulation extended. It is an honor to the publishers and I wish my name might remain as one of the publishers if only in name alone.

*Saturday 2d* — Went over to Council Bluffs with Mr Estabrook, his family and Judge Wakely. Went in the family Carriage. I found no taxes had been as yet assessed on our Iowa lands. Went alone upon the highest bluff by the burying ground where is a most splendid prospect, comprising in one view St Marys twelve miles below, Omaha Saratoga and Florance opposite. From this point I intend taking a birdseye view of the Trio City the Great City of the "Great West."

At Bluff City I met Hubbel Kelley who used to be one of my school and play mates when I was the age little Irwin is now and went to school on "Whipple Hill." We have met but once or twice since that time. I recognized him by the paculiarity of his voice. He has been here but a few days. Has come out West to seek a position. We had a long talk of old times.

I also met at the Bluffs S. M. Hall of Van Watters poetical Geographia fame. He had hunted for me all the morning at Omaha. Decided to return to Omaha where we met at five o'clock. Mr Hall got a buggy and we had the finest ride imaginable over the Saratoga platt. Mr. Hall thinks of purchasing a share if he can get one. He was delighted with the location.

Just as we crossed the ferry between four and five o'clock on our return from the Bluffs, the Steamer "Silver heels" came up with colors flying and a band of music which was animating in the extreme. She gives a dance to the Omaha people this evening taking them on board and going up to Florance by moonlight there finishing the dance and returning tomorrow morning.

The Steamer "Hannidal" came up during the night and was laying at our levee this morning. She had on board 200 Danes going to Join the Mormons. Her cargo was mostly lumber. We can now get pine siding for $50. per thousand. Planed and matched pine flooring $65. per thousand and pine shingles for $7.50 per thousand. This is cheaper than we ever expected to get pine lumber here, it will probably be the standard price and is cheap enough.

Among the wonders of Bluff City I saw an old Mormon 80 years of age who is sensible on all subjects but one, and that one is that he will live two or three hundred years yet and raise a large family of children. He is a widower now. He once married the widow of *Morgan* who was said to be murdered by the Masons during the great Anti-Masonic times which I can but just remember.

It is evening, a delightful one, and the closing in of a delightful day. The Silver heels has started up the river with her load of merry dancers. I had no desire to be one of the company still it is almost too pleasant to stay in the house. But I will go to bed, and see what a Morrow will bring forth.

*Sunday Morning May 3d* — The Steamer "Emma" came up during the night. I got up early and went down on board, found a friend of Mr Leidy whose acquaintance I made while here last fall. He tells me Mr. Leidy and family are at Davenport going to come around by St. Louis and bring up a ready made house. I shall be pleased to see him and his family. He seems an old acquaintance.

The Silverheels returned this morning and our levee looks quite business like with three steamers in port besides the Ferry Boat.

Just ready for church. Waiting for the second bell. Another steamer has just reached our levee making four here this morning. The "Silver heels" and "Hannibal" are starting down. From the window where I board we can see all the movements of the boats, Every arrival and departure. Mr. Estabrook coming in reports the last boat to be "the Asa Wilgus" and is going up as far as Sioux City..

Have been to church for the first time in Nebraska. Listened to a discourse by Mr. Gaylord. Old school Presbyterian. Like him very well.

But for the breeze which is blowing freshly from the South we should have a very hot day, as it is, it is the hottest of the Season. Immediately after dinner I took off my Coat and boots, put on slippers and wrapper, and straightened out on the lounge to take my ease. The door stood wide open and I had a fine view of the boats at the levee and up the River for miles. The view also comprised a greater part of Saratoga the most prominent feature of which was the spot I have selected near the spring. My *imagination* reared a little cottage there and peopled it with my family the children chasing gophers in the wild prarie grass. My wife reading a letter from the east and myself in the doorway in my easy chair watching the steamers coming up the river or with my spy glass peeping into Mr Estabrooks where I now am. This pleasant revery was broken up by Mr Hall's hurrying in for a share of Saratoga. The boat was to leave in twenty five minutes. He had the promise of one tomorrow but could not wait, I gave him mine and he counted me out the gold. It made a rich handfull for both of my hands. I shall get another tomorrow and hope to make a few dollars on it. Mr Hall left in a hurry to return with a house.

*Monday, 4th*  Waited around town for the arrival of the Mail which was a heavy one. It brought nothing for me. Tried to find a share of Saratoga at my own price. Think I shall get one for a little less than the one I sold.

This evening had a fine April shower accompanied with thunder and lightning. Spent the evening in drawing plans for my business house or place. At bed time the Steamer Emigrant came in from St Louis.

*Tuesday 5th*  Finished drawing my plans and went up to Saratoga to meet the Surveyors, but did not find them. Selected two lots for men to build on, who had just come in on that boat. Returned to Omaha just before noon and as usual repaired at once to the Post office. Got two papers an Express and Republic from Robert. Met Mr Cook who told me he had taken out letters for me and given them to Mr. Estabrook. When Mr E. came down to dinner he was disposed to have a little sport with me as I had been complaining so long about not getting letters, but the fact of my having heard he had the letters prevented the anticipated sport at My expence. One letter was from Brother Frank another enclosed one from my wife son and daughter each all of which was read with the deepest interest and proved very exilerating, Inspiring me with renewed energy. Answered letters in the afternoon.

*Wednesday 6th*  According to previous arangements hired a team to go down after my fence posts. Found them not touched. The proprietor of the mill sent me word once they would not be done as first promised, but would be done this day sure. I had hired a team. Been to all the expence and without gaining anything. This is characteristic of business in Nebraska. We want more prompt enerjetic working business men here than we have. It is just the place for such men to make money.

I do not expect now to get my posts as I will not go after them again or pay more for them delivered than I was to get them for at the Mail. It is getting late for a garden and I can do without a fence at present.

My trip to the mill was not wholly without interist as we saw some sights new to me. A prarie squirrel, a snake five feet long and a wild turkey. When we saw the turkey we were on the bottoms near the mill in the timber. It was a large gobbler and ran across the road ahead of us and up the bank. If I had had a shotgun I could have killed it. Fired four charges from my revolver at him. The distance was to far to have the balls take effect even if they had hit him. At the mill they informed us the wild turkeys were pleanty in the vicinity. Could hear them every morning about daylight. What a chance for Sporting Wild ducks are as pleanty as sparrows in the east.

About dark this evening the steamer "Washington City" came in three weeks from St Louis. Is a lower Mississippi boat and too large for the upper trade. There is some talk here this evening about purchasing it and keeping it as a hotel at our levee. The boat had on 50,000 feet lumber and some shingles, also a good supply of passengers 75 of which are bound to St Johns a Catholic colony near Sioux City to which place their fare is paid. The captain refuses to go farther and the passengers insist he must or refund their mony. What the result will be we cannot tell.

*Thursday 7* This days mail brought me a letter and two papers from Mr. Adams. The Republic and the Advocate. I think Mr Robe's hits Mr Lathrop rather hard. Answered Roberts letter and attended a meeting of the Sulphur Spring Land Co. The Company refused to ratify the proposition accepted from me by the donating Committy, on the ground that they had refused heretofore by a vote to donate any lots in the block from which I made my selections. They were pleased with my project and proposition and appointed Mr. Wm. G. Brown to negotiate with me on even more liberal terms in some other quarter. I refuse however to negotiate on *any* terms as I have now abandoned the project entirely and am glad the matter has taken the turn it has.

Purchased a share of Saratoga to replace the one I let Mr Hall have. Made something (#oll.) by the operation. Agreed to go over the river in the morning and set some men to work on, and superinted the building of a large flat-boat for ferrying over teams and wood for the brick makers. The flatboat is for the Company who furnish one thousand cord of wood for the brick men. The Company have contracted 2,000,000 brick to be made this season.

Owing to the absence of Mr. Tuttle the drawing is again posponed and will not come off until next Thursday the 14th. No further postponement will be made even if Mr Tuttle should not arrive. The steamer Washington was bought today for $15,000 for a hotel.

*Friday, 8.* During last night we had a fine Thunder shower. This morning it is clear and warm the wind blowing a gale from the South. The wind has blowed harder today than any day since I have been here. Still it has been oppressively hot all day and by noon the dust began to fly which together with the glaring sun and hot air from the oven down south has made it very unpleasant out of doors. The ferry boat has not ventured out until since sundown so that it was not possible to go over to see about the flat-boat. The ferry boat being delayed has prevented our receiving a mail today.

*Saturday, 9.* — The south wind which went down with the sun last evening changed about and this morning was in the north. By nine o'clock it was in the north west and blew nearly as hard as yesterday. The ferry boat only made one trip for the mail and that with difficulty. Went up to Saratoga. Found men at work grading Pacific avenue down the beach on to the bottom. After dinner signed papers for one of the gift Lots on Saratoga Avenue and assisted Mr Brown in preparing for the drawing. I think I never witnessed such a change in the weather under a bright sun. Yesterday the thermometer went up to 80. Today it is almost freezing cold making a fire necessary for comfort, still the sun is shining as bright as it did yesterday, the change is owing to the wind being in a different quarter.

Saturday night has come again. It is to me the most lonesome Evening of the week and one which I long to be at home to spend. I must not dwell to much upon home for there will doubtless be many long weeks before I can again be with my Family.

Mr Warner sold two lots which he paid $110. For not quite a year ago for $600. Such business will pay.

*Sunday, 10.* — The wind has blown but little today still it is cold and a fire very comfortable. Wrote during the forenoon to Irwin and Sophia. After lunch rode up to Saratoga with Mr. Estabrook and family after which I wrote Sister Sarah. Just as I finished the letter some Indians came to the house with two ponies. The Indians were acquainted with Mr Estabrook. The party consisted of a chief his squaw and two of his children the oldest a squaw as large as her mother the other a boy about 14 years old. The chiefs name is Corax. Belongs to the Pawne tribe and is their *War* chief. He is the best looking Pawnie I have seen. Is six feet tall and well proportioned. Speaks very little english. He says "Mr Estabrook good Semokaman" meaning white man. The chief had on mocasins leggins breech-cloth and a large Buffalo skin held on by a band across his sholders. This completed his clothing. He carried a large bow and quiver of arrows, ornaments in his ears and on his head. He let his Robe fall down to his waist leaving his back breast and arms perfectly naked giving him a noble look as he stood up erect, his hands crossed in front of him. What he could not speak in english he made known by signs which were made the most gracefull and almost seemed to speak, they were so plain any one could understand them. He was given some supper on a separate table after which he called in his squaws and boy to eat, then went away. After tea we were in the parlor. The family were singing and Mr E. playing on his violin when Mr Chief walked in and took his seat on the lounge with the rest. What a contrast and the same time how noble he looked.

*Monday, 11.* — This day was advertised for the sale of Park lots to complete the Capitol. The sale did Not Commence until 4 o'clock P. M. Six lots were sold for some over $6000, which was not what was expected they would bring. Accordingly the sale was adjourned to some future day when the balance will be sold. Mr. Warner wishing to attend the sale nothing else was done. Steamer Admiral up from St Louis.

Our Chief and his family were admited into the kitchen last night where they slept on the floor.

*Tuesday, 12.* — Devoted the forenoon to going over into Iowa on business connected with the flat boat. Afternoon rainy. In accordance with a previous arangement went up at 10 P. M. to sit up with Mr Goodwill who is very low with typhoid fever. Other persons were there and my services were not required. Returned as I went, in the midst of a drenching rain, which wet my clothing through to my skin in many place.

*Wednesday, 13.* — Not well this morning. Have symptoms of my old complaint. It has rained all night and is dark and lowry but warm. Vegitation looks fine.

The Chief and his family are still in the vicinity. Corax has swapped his Buffalo Robe for a blanket. Got on a shirt, old vest and a hat with a red band around it. He is neither white man or indian in dress now, His mongrel suit takes away much of his noble looks.

The steamer Edinburgh came in this noon with a large lot of lumber, and as the boats all are full of passengers, at bed time felt well as usual except somewhat homesick. Weather more cool tonight.

*Thursday, 14.* — Disagreeably wet and cold. Did not leave the house until ten o'clock when Mr. Campbell, late book keeper for Cutter & Deforest, of Buffalo called on me. He came in yesterday on the Edenburgh. Is boarding at the steamboat lately purchased for a Hotel. I went down to the boat with him and found Mr De Puy wife and infant daughter. My presence cheered up Mr De Puy although Mr Campbell said he dreaded to meet me. Mr De Puy looks old and broken spirited. Has placed every thing in Campbells hands who manages for him and is his financier and director. It was quite a pleasant interview with DePuy and Campbell, seemed like home again.

Afternoon spent with Saratoga Co arranging the drawing. A strong west wind has prevented the Ferry from crossing until near night. A mail then came over and I received the May noumbers of the "Home" and "Casket" still I do not receive letters from home as I should. I ought to have one every week as regular as the weeks come. I have thus far only received one a month.

*Friday, 15.* — Spent an hour or two posting up Mr Campbell and DePuy, the balance of the day until ten at night assisted in arranging the ballots for the Saratoga drawing.

*Saturday, 16.* — The Steamer "Omaha" came in this morning. Discharged her freight for this place and passed up on her way to Sioux City. Completed the ballots for the drawing about nine o'clock this evening. Having been kept busy for the past few days I have felt the most contented since I came here.

A large wolf had the impudence to come over the bluff into town this morning about nine o'clock and probably would have killed a young colt a few hours old had he not been discovered. He left followed closely by a couple of dogs who chased him out on the prarie.

About noon our Chief Corax left for the Pawnee Camp some Sixty Miles west. The last day of his stop in town he pitched his tent within four rods of Mr Estabrooks. When I came to dinner I watched them pack their ponies. The chief and his son held the ponies while the squaws done the work of packing and taking down the tent. As I stood looking at them I thought squaws were just the persons to have when one wants to move, as they will make such small parsels of their effects which at first sight would seem sufficient for a waggon load. We were at dinner when they left. Corax came to the door to bid us good-by. He had taken of his dress in which he tried to appear like a white man, and looked better than ever. His only change in dress which differed from what he wore on his arrival was a banditti hat and a fire red blanket bordered with a strip of white about six inches wide. His quiver was hung across his shoulders and his bow was in his hand. His broad chest and brawny arms were naked except two or three bands of some bright metal which ornamented the latter. At the door he said "Corax, Estabrook, Pawnee house," then put his hands to gether and shook them, pointed to the west. To me he said "Semokeman Pawnee house" and made the motions and signs as before. His signs ment that if we would come to his house at the Pawnee village he would treat us kindly. Give us corn and meat and a nice tent to sleep under when the sun went down. When I went out from dinner I could see the party going up the bluff out of town Corax ahead the squaws leading the ponies and the boy behind.

Corax is about forty years old. It is said of him that he has probably scalped more white people crossing the plains than any Pawnee of the tribe. He is however a most noble specimen of the Indian, and is at peace and friendly with the whites. The Pawnees south of the Platt River claim the lands in a certain vicinity and do not allow the whites to settle there unless they are paid for the lands. They are about making a treaty. The Indians have been greatly wronged, and as a general thing when there is Indian depredations the Whites are the first aggressors.

The Pawnees were once numerous and very powerfull, and most to be dreaded of all the western indians. In their wars with the Sioux and their intercourse with the Whites they have become as week as they were once powerfull, and are the most low filthy and degraded race in the west. They use no fire-arms. There only weopens are the hatchet and bow and arrows. Their arrows are steel pointed, and the same arrow that is used to kill a squirrel will kill a Buffalo. I have perhaps said enough about the Pawnees. Their relics are on every hand and it will be long years before they are entirely efaced by civilization. Among the curiosities of this place is the remains of old fort Crogan.

*Sunday, 17* — A delightfull day. Immediately after breakfast I started off alone to indulge in one of my most favorite enjoyments that is a Sabbath day walk entirely by myself. I had a very pleasant time indeed, the grass is up sufficient to give the prarie such a color as I never saw it dressed in before, which color is pea green. The sun shone bright but there was sufficient breeze to prevent its being too warm. I went up to Saratoga where I had not been for a week. Great changes had taken place in the way of buildings comenced and the grading of Pacific Avenue. Went up to the lot I have selected and plucked some flowers two of which I will send to Sophia, in my first letter to her. Crossed the platt or table land from my lot by going west on Saratoga Avenue over the bluff to Mr. Tuttles farm. Here I found garden vegetables far advanced and two men Joseph McNeal and Wm. Pitcher from Cooperstown at

work in the garden. Like all new countries before the people get settled
or have time to make places of worship there is but little regard paid
to the Sabbath. Br. Cook is often prevented from attending church
in consequence of the arrival of a Steamer with freight for Mr Rogers
which must be received and charges paid or the goods would be taken
back on the boat. From Mr. Tuttle's farm I returned to Omaha just in
time for my dinner. The Steamer "John Warner" had arrived from St
Louis. After dinner took a ride with the General and family. Returned to
an early supper. During the evening the steamer "New Monongahalia"
came up.

*Monday 18* — Commenced the business of the day by revising Saturdays
work, after which went up to Saratoga. Returned half past eleven. Got
a letter from home, dated May 3d and mailed the 4th. Enclosed was
one for Miss Augusta and one for me from wife, son and daughter. I
wish I could receive one every week. I presume my last letter is received
this day. Mr Tuttle is still absent which fact keeps me undecided as
to my future course of business. This evening about dark the Steamer
"Spread Eagle" passed up without stopping. She was in imploy of the
fur company or the government and her only load was supplies for the
North.

*Tuesday, 19* — This morning we have four boats in, the The "A. C.
Goddin" "Silver Heels" and "Emma" from St Louis and the "Omaha"
on her return from up Country. Mr. Goodwill died this morning at
one o'clock. His death is a great blow to Omaha and Saratoga. He was
one of the first pioneers and kept the first house of entertainment in
the place, known as the "*big six*". His doors have ever been open to the
Emigrant, and although he he kept a public house but a short time, he
was always at the boats, to look after the interest of new comers and
give up his own bed while he would take the floor. He has been twice
a member of the Territorial Council, and at his death was Receiver of
taxes for the County and city, was Alderman of Omaha and Chairman
of the Executive Committe of the "Sulphur Spring Land Co. His whole
energies were at work to build up this region which has made others
wealthy while he has worked more and accumulated less. The rise on his

property here has however left his family in comfortable circumstances. The loss of his only son, a boy about 14 years of age, last winter we think has had the effect to so wear on his mind as to impair his bodily health. Immediately after breakfast went up to Saratoga. Returned to the Company Meeting and we commenced drawing for lots, and waked until ten at night when we adjourned until morning.

*Wednesday – 20* — Continued the drawing untill about noon at which time we had drawn twelve lots to a share, tho the number dessignated for the first drawing.

After dinner preparations were being made by the "odd Fellows" and others to attend Mr Goodwills funeral. The attendance bade fare to be a large one. I accordingly repaired to Saratoga and looked out and staked some of the lots I had drawn. Came home, right tired, to a late supper.

*Thursday, 21.* — This day has mostly been consumed at a meeting of the Sulphur Spring Land Co. At which I was elected Chairman of the Executive Committee, to fill the vacancy caused by the death of Mr Goodwill. The most important duties I shall have to perform is the making of and executing Contracts with persons receiving donation lots. The whole business of donations is in my hands. I objected to accepting at first but I have made myself so familliar with the ground, I was selected in spite of my opposition. Received a letter from Dr. Gray under date of May 8th. Mr. Gridley made his appearance here this morning. Came in on the Emma yesterday.

*Friday, 22.* — Spent the forenoon in arranging the papers of the Executive Committee and donating eight lots. Afternoon went up to Saratoga. Called on a Mr Smiley from Ohio, who has just got into his house brought with him from Pittsburgh. The company gave him one of the best locations on the corner of Audubon and fifteenth Streets. It commands a most delightful view of the river, Omaha City and surrounding country. One consideration of Mr Smiley's getting the location he did was his large family consisting of one Son and five Daughters the Daughters all marriageable. The oldest is east still as a teacher. The next wishes to teach hear. I presume we shall have a School in operation by fall. There is now as many as twenty small children living in Saratoga where ten days ago there was none.

*Saturday, 23.* — An excessively warm day with a strong wind from the South making it very unpleasant out of doors on account both of heat and dust.

This days mail brought me a pile of reading matter, papers from New-york, Buffalo and Auburn also Mr. Browns paper from Kansas and a letter from Mr. Brown and one from Harriet. The papers were very opportune as they helped to pass away this hot dusty day. From the Auburn paper I learn what Dr. Gray had before written me that Mrs. Woodruff and Brennan were indicted. I cannot see what will prevent their being found guilty although Frank writes doubtfull. The letter from Harriet was partly to me and part to Cook and in answer to one I wrote asking for my pen which was enclosed. They were well even to "red head."

Mr. Brown in his letter still urges me to come to Lawrence, he says "Kansas is the place to make money *Sure as you are born.*" If I fail to get into business suited to me here I shall go to Lawrence. Mr Tuttle is expected by the first boat. A letter received by the Teller of the Bank this day states that he, Mr Tuttle, is on his way, the letter was written from Illinois. I consider that my not meeting him here has been a great disappointment to me, and I am tired remaining comparatively idle and daily expecting his return. Mr. Tuttle writes that his wife has a son that will be able to take the tellership of the Bank in a short time and that the present tellers services will not be required long. (At this moment I am interrupted particulars on another page.)

Had I known all the facts communicated in Mr Browns letter, at the time of My first arrival here this spring I should undoubtedly have felt remarkably uneasy when I was complaining of ill health. The facts are these as it seemes from Mr Browns letter from which I quote: "Mrs Brown, it seems, had the *small pox* on board the steamer as we came up the river. She Communicated it to her sisters who are yet confined with it one of whom we consider dangerous. Mrs B had it very light of course the Varialoid." If I recollect aright I wrote while coming up the river, something of Mrs. Brown's not being well, having weak eyes and a good deal of fever so that she did not go to the table at all times. No one however thought of its being the Small pox in any form. The disease must have been communicated to a great number among so many passengers. Had I know the facts I have no doubt I should have been down sick on first arrival, as my indisposition at that time would have been attributed to the symptoms of small pox instead of a cold which was the case. "All is well that ends well."

Four young men who set out with a waggon and a span of Mules on the 16th April on an exploring toor, have returned with a glowing descriptions of the Country along the *Running Water*. I listened perfectly captivated for an hour to their accounts of the game they saw and the incidents by the way. They staked out their claim and propose locating a town to be called Junction Rapids. It is at the junction of two steams forming the Running Watter. The region in which they traveled has never been explored and was thought unsafe on account of the *Puncoes* a desperate band of Indians. The party however met with no obsticles in the form of Indians. I mean to get a full description of their discoveries.

This evening I went up to Cooks to give him the papers to read. There I found some Omaha squaws trading. One was called "old Mary." She spoke five languages, has been to school five years at St Josephs and been to the city of Washington. With her were the two widows of Logan Fontenelle the chief who was murdered a few years since while on a buffalo hunt, by a war party of Sioux. In my diary of last year I wrote that Logan Fontinelle was burried on the present site of Saratoga near the sulphur spring. Old Mary says that is a mistake. The grave in question, which is so singularly made and surrounded with polings, is where the daughter of "Young Elk" was buried. Logan Fontenelle was buried at Belleview by the side of his father of the same name who died very old, and was for many years chief of the Omahas. The elder Fontenelle was succeeded by Young Elk who was a great chief. After Young Elk the younger Fontenelle was made chief. Since his death the Omahas have been without a Chief.

Old Mary has agreed to make a pair of mcasins for my children. I gave her money to get beads. She says there is a coal mine about twenty miles from the Black bird hills which has not been claimed. She says she will show white folks where it is for pay. She says white folks come to her house they get breakfast dinner and supper for nothing. Indians don't charge fifty cents a meal. All is free.

*Sunday, 24.* — Have written all under date of 22d and 23d this morning. The interruption I received a short time since was caused by the marriage of the girl that works here and the hired man. They were married by Judge Wakely and have gone over into Iowa to visit an Uncle. Will be back Tuesday. Said Judge Wakely is of the Northern district lately appointed, is from Wisconsin. He has been stoping here for a few days. Is about my age. This is the first couple he ever married. He was considerably embarrised but done it up strong and quick. Being his first experience in Marrying he gave his fee to the bride. They are a fine clever couple. Thus ends the one hundredth page of this diary.

Have just returned from a long walk with Mr Warner up to Saratoga. On our return we saw a rattlesnake in the road which we killed with a cane. I cut off the rattles and will enclose them in my first letter. About a hundred rods from where we killed the snake we found a much smaller rattlesnake which had been killed during the day. It had but two or three rattles. A short distance farther we saw four men apperantly killing a snake. When we came up we found a snake called here a blower. This one was as much as five feet long. They are spoted like a milk snake and perfectly harmless. I killed one on my return walk from Saratoga on Friday a fact I forgot to mention. The rattlesnake we killed tried to get away from us, and was not at all inclined to show fight but rattled furiously.

The steamer St Mary's stoped about noon and passed up with government stores. At Evening the steamer Mink painted nearly black and belonging to the Government came up and stoped for the night. She is bound for Fort Peer some seven hundred miles above this point up the Missourie. Her loading was Government supplies. Carries no freight or passengers for outsiders.

*Monday, 25* — A disagreeable rainy day. Received a letter from Robert with some very gratifying news for instance the renting of the house. The letter was a very interesting one. Some parts of it however did not make me feel very pleasant. When I went home to dinner found The

General and Augusta singing and playing "Rosalee the Prarie flower." What a sensation it created within me. I had never heard the first word of it since I left home. And I could imagine I heard Sophias voice in every line and word of it. How instantaniously I was transported to my family. Augusta was delighted with the music. She could sing and play "Rosalie the Prarie flower" in a half hour after it was received.

*Tuesday, 26* — Mr Brown's clerk being sick to day I have been in the office until three o'clock, then went up to Saratoga, found all moveing prosperously. During my walk up to Saratoga the steamer "Minnehaha" came in.

A bachelors dancing party came off this evening on board the Hotel steamer Washington City. The General being absent Augusta was intrusted to my care until Eleven o'clock at night. And for the first time in Omaha I went where there was an assemblage of Ladies. Of course I did join the party but went as a spectator and guardian of Augusta at the request of the family. A number of gentlemen came to me to be introduced to my little girl. She danced every set and when she left had four or five unfulfilled engagement. She was the best dancer in the room, and many were almost inclined to use physical force to prevent her leaving. On our way home her tongue flew very much as I have heard Sophia's at times.

The attraction of the party however to me was not Miss Augusta or her dancing. But as Jonathan Slick says "it was them grown up gals all finefied off with ribbons and laces, sidling and twisting around, their bare arms and naked necks making them look good enough to eat." After one or two cotillions more ladies came which I did not notice until they came out of the dressing room and took their seats. The fluttering of dresses in that direction caused me to look around, and didn't I stare some there sat a woman a perfect Degareotype of my wife in features, at a front view. I learned she was a Miss Clark a sister of a Mr Clark of the firm of Armstrong & Clark merchants in town. If I had belonged to the party I should have made her acquaintance. I shall endeavor to see her by daylight, and if she bares the resemblance as well as in the evening I shall try and get an introduction, as yet I have made but two calls in Omaha and those were on acquaintance.

*Wednesday, 27* — This day assisted Mr Wyman the present Post Master in putting up his presses and aranging his office. He had a new one direct from the Foundry and is going to establish a daily and weekly. I done some heavy lifting without any unpleasant results.

*Thursday, 28* — Finished putting up the presses about two o'clock, an hour previous to which Mr. Cockett came in to see me. He had arrived the day previous at evening in company with Mr. Tuttle. I spent the balance of the day with Mr Cockett went up to Saratoga with him and Mr Tuttle. Mr C. thinks Saratoga is just the place. During the day four more persons arrived from Cooperstown. Erastus Root, a Winslow and Short boy. Received a letter from Frank written the day before Cockett left.

 In the Evening called on Mr. Gridley of Buffalo who is stopping at Mr Kellums. He has been unwell since his arrival but is now about well again. Learned of the failure of John R. Lee & Co which much surprised me. The Steamer Alonzo Childs in.

*Friday 29* — Spent this day with Mr Cockett. Had a very pleasant time, afternoon rainy. Received papers from Brother Irwin. Steamer Sultan came in at bed time.

*Saturday 30* — passed this day as yesterday with Mr Cockett. Had also a short interview with Mr. Tuttle. The afternoon rainy. I am having the best of times with Mr Cockett. It seemes much like being with Frank. We talk up Cooperstown matters and I feel almost home again. Another batch of papers from Irwin.

*Sunday 31.* — Cool wet morning. Preaching was to come off at the "Central House" this forenoon the first in Saratoga notwithstanding the unpleasant weather I was bound to go up. The General got out his carriage for me and his little nephew, Augusta, and myself got in drove up to the "Hamilton House" took in Mr Cackett and went up to Saratoga. Just as we arrived at the Central House we found the Minister leaving some mistake had been made and the house was not ready and the weather prevented many from coming so the meeting is put off two weeks. By that time the Centra house will probably be completed ready to be opened to the public. It will be the best Hotel in Nebraska.

Three steamers have come up today. The "Hannibal" "Waucassa" and "Asa Wilgus" all loaded with passengers. You would be surprised to see the trains of emigrants that come across the country bound for the interior of this Territory Salt Lake and California some trains are a mile long. It would seem at this rate that the entire east would become depopulated.

A host of people from Herkimer county, friends of Mr Tuttle, came up on one of todays steamers. They are all men of means, are delighted with the country. Among the number is a noted clergimen who is in ectasies about this country.

After tea went up to the Hamilton House and took a stroll with Mr. Cockett. Went out of town about a mile and a half in a direction I had not been before. I was equally charmed with Mr. Cockett. We could not help remarking again and again, "I wish Frank was here" to enjoy this treat with us. It was dark when we returned. Halted just at dusk where an Emigrant train to Callifornia were pitching their tents. They had eleven covered wagons and families a supply of horses and three hundred head of cattle. The men were some of them watching the cattle others putting down the tents. The children gathering fuel while the women were getting supper. The made some as fine biscuit as I ever saw baking them in an old fashioned "bake-kittle." Fried bacon coffee and warm cakes with molasses constituted the bill of fare. Oil cloths were spread on the ground and the table-ware arranged much as it would be on a table. Not receiving an invitation to sup with them we did not stop to see how they arranged themselves to eat, but presume the took seats on the ground. Their supper smelled delisious and would be a luxury to some families here who live on "cut straw and molasses." Called at Mr Tuttles House where two of the families from Herkimer are to stop, and had a pleasant interview with the clergyman and Governor Izard. Mr Tuttle has purchased the governors house, and occupy it until his house at Saratoga is finished.

*Monday June 1, 1857* — Remained in the office attending to the donation of lots this forenoon, received a letter from my wife and one from

Frank. Mr. Cockett bought a small Cincinnati house fifteen feet square, brought up by Mr. Gridley, for $200. After dinner got a team and went up with the first load and selected our lot. Mr. Cockett and Myself are to own the building and lot jointly. Mr C purchased the building and I am to finish it for my share. While our teamster was after the second load, we looked out and went on our lots which proved better than we had expected.

Walked out in the evening after supper and talked up business, also our old business operations in Buffalo. Did not separate until after ten o'clock.

*Tuesday, 2* — Spent the forenoon with Mr Tuttle and Mr Gridley. The mail brought me a letter from one of cousin Benjamins girls who is at school in Indiana. Mr. Cockett gone over to the Bluffs.

After dinner went up to Saratoga. Sawed out ten oak posts and set five of them as part of the foundation for the office. Hired a carpenter to comence tomorrow to help me put up the building. Was very tired when I got home to supper. After tea went up town and chatted an hour with Mr Cockett who had returned from the Bluffs. The Seamer Admiral in from St. Louis.

*Wednesday 3* — Put up the frame for the office. Had hard days work and returned at night very tired.

*Thursday 4* — Assisted the carpenter on the building donated lots for a church and parsonage. The doner a G. W. Skinner of Herkimer Co N. Y. a friend of Mr Tuttle, is a Unitarian will preach Sunday in the Central House Saratoga and at Omaha in the evening. The Steamer D. A. January is in bound up the river.

*Friday 5* — Worked on the building same as yesterday do not feel well to day in consequence of sore tongue and mouth. Have the Steamers "New Monongahala" and "John Warner" in from St. Louis.

Before going up to Saratoga I bade Mr. Cockett good by as he was to leave on a steamer toward Nome. My walk to Saratoga was a very lonely one after parting with Mr. Cockett. We have had the pleasantest kind of a time since he has been here. I found him almost equal to Frank for fun and a joke, and could not but be loth to part with him I hope some good to us both will grow out of his visit to this place.

*Saturday 6* — Did not go up to Saratoga untill after dinner. Had a long chatt with Mr. Tuttle. He talks large for me, and if one half he tells me turns out right I shall be satisfyed. Our town is honored with a number of Railroad men from the east. They are large portly silver-haired gold-headed-cane gentlemen who are posted on R. R. Matters.

Saratoga is growing rapidly every day adds a new house and some days two are commenced. If I remain a whole day down to Omaha I see a marked change in improvements. In one months time I shall hardly be able to keep track of the improvements. I shall be obliged to call on the company for a horse to ride soon or it will take my wholl time to look afer affairs, of the company which I am expected to do. We have Steamers "Omaha" and "Edenburg" in today. The annual June rise of the Missourii has commenced. Has risen some two feet will probably continue to rise untill the last of the month. Then gradually subside untill the fall rains set in. During the June rise the freights on the river are the lowest of the Season. The June Rise is occasioned by snows from the Mountains which do not commence to melt before the hot weather sets in in this Latitude.

*Sunday 7* — An excessively warm day. A strong wind is all that makes the heat enduable. The themometer ranges from 96 to 100. The incessant wind we have here is a great luxury in summer.

Br. Cook and myself walked up to Saratoga to hear the first sermon in the place. It was delivered by a Mr Bergen a Prespyterian the text was: "Deliver unto Ceazar the things that ar Ceazars and unto God the things that are Gods." The discourse was a very good one and delivered in the Central house our unfinished hotel. In going up and returning we stoped at the Sulphur spring and took a drink, it was the first time Mr. Cook had seen the spring. This afternoon at three o'clock Mr. Skinner a Unitarian, is to preach at the Central house. It is too warm for me to walk up again. I accordingly devote my time to writing and keeping cool as possible.

The excessive heat of the day has kept us up late enjoying the cool evening out in the steps hanging out of the windows and watching the lighting for diston thunder clouds.

*Monday 8* — Remained in Omaha during the forenoon answering letters and attending to other business. Afternoon went up to Saratoga and spent the balance of the day in showing the gift lots to different parties. Returned — very much fatiegued by the walk in the hot sun. The steamer "Emma" up from below bound farther up the river.

*Tuesday 9* — Went up to Saratoga directly after breakfast. On my way I killed the largest snake I ever saw alive except such as I have seen in shows. It was six feet long and as larg around as my arm. They are a species of snake resembling in color and shape an anaconda or boa-constrictor. When angry they make a blowing noise and it is said the breath they blow out if inhaled in large quantities produces a very nausea sickness for a short time. This I am not inclined to credit. They never bite and are nout in the least venemous. The blower is a great distroyer of the rattlesnake. Kills them whenever they can find thim, by circuling them within their folds and crushing them to death. By this same mode they destroy small animals which they swallow whole to satisfy hunger. The one I killed I think could have swallowed a small cat.

Assisted about half the day in the office in putting on the ruff boards. The balance of the day showing up and donating lots. Had as many as twenty calls, at one time five carriages and twelve or fifteen persons including ladies. At one time I rode this way with a party, at another walked that half a dozen following me and looking up lots to get for the building on them.

When the five carriages at one time were waiting on me one person calling me this way and another that. All doing their best to get the most desirable location. I thought of Brothers Frank and Irwin. They would say "the kite is going it now" and it did sail up some. But there was a little too much tail to it wishing to go different ways so it did not go out of sight.

My position in the company makes me acquainted with every person before he locates in the place. And I trust my attention to them wins their friendship which I think will do me no harm if it is not of *real* service to me. My office will do to go into this week and I shall get all the agency business of the setters and also their influence. This may not count at once but if I can manage to get along for the present, I believe I shall succeed in doing first rate business and be one of them in the city of Saratoga. Three months today since I left home or rather since I left Buffalo.

*Wednesday 10* — Assisted in laying the floor to my office at Saratoga returning to Omaha found the steamer "Joseph Oglesby" in, one of the largest boats ever coming to this place. Being her first trip she gave a free party to the citizens. It is customary for every boat making its first trip of the season to come prepared to give a dance and they get up some splendid affairs all free. I had only attended one and that was as a spectator and company for Miss Augusta. It was at this time I saw Miss Clark which so much resembles my wife. — Since which time I have not had a sight of said lady. Accordingly I decided I would saunter down to the boat after the dance should commence and see what I could see. As I started out about nine o'clock I met Br. Cook who by invitation accompanied me to the boat. I told him I was going to the boat to see a lady. Cook laughed and said something about how good calico looked in Nebraka. Before going on the boat I told Cook to take notice of a certain lady I would point out to him, if she was there, and see if he ever saw any one that looked like her before. The lady in question was on the floor in a cotilion about the center of the cabin, when we went in. I pointed in the direction Cook noticed her at once and remarked "crackie that is Mate exactly." The more he looked the more natural Mates representative appeared. We stoped long enough to see two cotillons then left thinking of home, and more of the folks at home.

*Thursday 11* — Mr Warner has been sick for some five days with dysentery. Not so sick however as to prevent him moving around a little. He is as nervious as I am and more old-madeish. He determined to start for home this morning. I spent the forenoon settling up his business and getting him ready for a start, accompanied him to the boat, and bade him good-by. We were old acquaintance and since we have been here we have slept together, and it seemed rather sad to have him leave particular on account of his health and gave me some unpleasant reflections the balance of the day, about how I should fare in this Territory were I taken sick.

After dinner went up to Saratoga. Have had the least wind and warmest sun to day since I have been in the Territory. It has been a hot one. Received a letter from Sister Sarah written at East Pembroke, where she was with the children.

We have two boats in today the "Watassa" and the "E. A. Ogden.

*Friday 12* — Spent the day as usual at Saratoga. Donated five lots to Mr. Tuttles friends who are to commence at once to build. They are all fine people with fine families. One is from Little Falls. Has a shoe store there and his wife is extensively in the milinery business. Mr Gray, the gentlemans name, has taken the next but one lot to mine. Will put up a store sufficient for his and his wifes business, and large enough to live overhead. He will then return for his goods and family. The others have their families with them.

This evening have spent with Br. Cook. He has leased one of Mr Warners lots for four years. Intends to build and send for his family at once. He has a good situation is doing well and has leased at a great bargain. We have talked over our chances &c of getting our families here until I feel extra lonesome and homesick tonight. I go to bed to sleep for the first time since I came to this territory, alone. I am glad to be without a bed-fellow unless it be of a different sex from what I have had since I left Buffalo. I am however getting somewhat weaned and feel a good deal like an old bachaler.

The steamers in to-day are the, "Dan Converse" and Moses Greenwood.

*Saturday 13* — Having an opportunity to ride I left Saratoga at four o'clock after laboring in a very hot sun as long as I felt disposed. My carpenter has at least one or two more days work on the office before

It will be completed. The balance of the work including painting &c I shall probably do myself.

Arriving at Omaha went direct to the P. O. got one paper and three letters. The paper was from Irwin one of the letters was for John L. Beadle mailed in Ohio. I put it back writing on the envelope a few lines for said John to call on me perhaps we are cozins. One of the other letters was from Mr McKim and the third from wife under date of May 30th. The latter letter was the greatest Saturday nights treat I have had in a long time. I read and re-read the letter and sets my wits to work to decide what was best that was feasible, and what that was feasible was best. After tea went up to consult with Cook. He has his arrangements nearly completed is only awating the result of one decision which will come off next tuesday, if favorable, of which I have no doubt it will be. He will send the same day for his family to come as soon as possible. I presume *his* family will be here in four or five weeks. This makes me more anxious than ever. I am in hopes something will turn soon which will enable me to send for my family. I am tired of this bachelor life.

We have had the finest sunset this evening I ever beheld, since which a storm has been gathering, and at this moment the wind seems as though it would demolish the dwelling while the lightning and thunder is incessant and the rain comes in torrents. I will stop and go to bed as the storm makes me feel weak so good night wife and children.

*Sunday morning before breakfast June 13.* — Feel very much prostrated this morning. The storm last evening compelled me to close the windows, thus preventing fresh air from coming into the room, and this morning is still hot and sultry, making me feel some sixty years old. The storms of last night were the worst I ever experienced In this Territory. The thunder and lightning being the most severe and incessant. One storm would spend its fury and subside until I would get into a drowse. Then another would come up if possible more severe than the last. This was continued until after midnight before I got to sleep. The steamers of yesterday were the "Alonso Child" and "Min-nehaha."

*Four O'clock P.M.* — Thus far have I spent the day in writing excepting while at breakfast and what time I occupied in bathing and changing my linen. It has been a most excessively warm day I never saw so warm weather after such a Thunder shower one could almost see the corn and vegitables grow. We have hotter weather here than in Buffalo, but almost sure to have a wind. Today it has blown a hurrycane but without the wind one would almost melt. The thermometer ranges to 95 today. Think of that for the 19th of June. I have engaged my potatoes for next winter at fifty cents a bushel cheap enough as yet.

*Monday 15* — Last night was equal to the previous for its severe storms of Thunder lightning and rain. This Morning warm as usual walked up to Saratoga remained until a severe Thunder storm came up the middle of the afternoon. Rode down in the omnibus. Found a letter in the office from Irwin with a scrap from Mate.

During the storm of Saturday night a horse was killed by lightning in town. Last week a new and large church was commenced here by the Presbyterians (old school) yesterday they organized and elected officers a Mr Barcalow President of the "Nemaha Valley Bank" and E. F. Cook were elected Deacons. I think Cook will make a good Decon he is doing well here.

*Tuesday 16* — This morning cool and cloudy. Occasional showers of rain with very high north winds prevents my going up to Saratoga today. Cook has this day sent the money for Lib to come to Omaha. She has had no intimation of it and will be happily disappointed. She will stop a short time at Hatts and probably be here about the first of August. I have had the blues some today wrote a long letter to wife and laid it by to add to tomorrow. The Steamer "Florence" in tonight.

*Wednesday 17* — Still windy, cloudy and cold. Read over my letter written yesterday and decided not to send it. It was to much under the influence of the blues when it was written so will burn it. Spent the day calling at the bank chatting with Tuttle, at the Printing offices and on the Deacon. Been a very disagreeable cold day raining every twenty minutes in regular April shower fassion. A church fair in town this eveng. I dont attend, want of capital.

*Thursday 18* — Clear and pleasant. Went up to Saratoga found two families occupying my office. They had come in on the 15th and were occupying their waggons the severity of the storm had compelled them to take reffuge in the office. The office had no door in front and only the ruff boards on so that they were obliged to put up their tent cloths to keep off the rain. The stove pipe was put out of one of the front windows. The women expected a worse storm when I came and saw the state of affairs. But I could have no objections of course not! Assisted in putting on the composition roofing until tea time took some dry bread custard and tea to stay my stomach until I should reach Omaha, having went without my dinner. After tea Mr Cook came down for me to go to the fair which was to be continued this evening said he would pay the expences. Fixed up and went, where I was in hopes to meet Miss Clark. The room was crowded so as to make it almost impossible to get around. Miss Clark was not there. There was however a good supply of ladies. One thing Omaha cannot boast of and that is good looking women. I believe my folks ordinery looking as they are wuld create an impression in town. The best looking of the ladies were the Miss Smiley's of Saratoga of course Saratoga was always noted for its fine looking ladies even in N.Y. and the same is true of Saratoga Nebraska. We have the Steamer Silver heels in today.

*Friday 19* — Went up to Saratoga and completed putting on the ruffing alone finished about three P. M. Completed the day by examining the improvements in town and seeing that all was being done according to agreement. Returned with a good appetite for my supper having fasted since breakfast. The Steamer "Watassa" in from St. Josephs.

*Saturday 20* — Do not feel well to day will not go to Saratoga. Have spells of dizzyness in my head attribute it to my last two days work on the roof in the hot sun and being up late the last two nights. The night of the fair I left with Mr Tuttle went over to the bank and did not leave until one o'clock. We got engaged in talking and did not notice the time. Last evening was at a meeting of citizens called to take into consideration the propriety of issuing city script to complete the capitol.

Quite an excitement in town on the arrival of the first circus in

Nebraska. It is to exhibit this afternoon and evening. Circuses it seems keeps pace with other emigration. Undoubtedly it will be crowded as allmost every one will go even to the Indians. Amusements are scarce here and circus will draw.

After dinner went up to the circus ground got into the crowd and was drawn in. Every body was there I did not know there was so many people in this County. The performance was much better than I expected it would be. A little girl about the size of Sophia went into a cage with a leopard. It was a dangerous looking sight. I went to the circus more to change the state of my feeling produced by my physical indisposition. By about tea time my dizzy spells had changed to hot flashes severe pain in my back and head. What would I not give to be home or with my family at this time. I am going up to have Cook come down and stay with me tonight. The Steamer Admira up from St. Louis.

*Sunday 21* — Had a miserable night. Cook came down, to stay with me. Judge Black however coming home with the general to stay all night, I expected I should be obliged to share my bed with him, and Cook did not stop. He might have done as the Judge slept on the lounge. I was fidgity all night. Could not sleep well. If I ever get my family around me again I hope I shall not be obliged to be absent from them so long again. Do not feel any better this morning not having rested well. After breakfast went up and got a box of sidledtz powders, going to doctor myself some to-day.

The day has passed and I think I feel somewhat improved, although not as I would wish to feel. Will not however complain unless I am worse than at present, being away from my family magnifies my ailments. Nothing of importance to fill this page.

*Monday 22* — Nothing of note today. Kept quiet in order to favor medicins taken. In the afternoon set in Cooks shop while he purchased lumber for his house. The steamers up to day are the 'Asa Wilgus, D. H. Morton and Emygrant.

*Tuesday 23* — Very warm rainy morning. Omaha Indians in town to buy horses preparatory to going on a Buffalo hunt. Mr. Estabrook offered them his poney. Had Augusta ride him that he might show off to better advantage. The saddle being put on loosely it slipped around under the Pony throwing Augusta to the ground when the Pony was going down hill at full speed. No harm was done however. And the General could blame no one as he put on the saddle himself. We were all somewhat frightened.

Before Dinner time it cleared off and in the afternoon I went up to Saratoga had not been there since friday. In so short a time even I saw a marked change, in new buildings raised. All at Saratoga were becoming anxious about me. Donated four lots and returned feeling perfectly well again. In the evening attended a preliminary political meeting. The General is a candidate for Congress. I am using my little influence for him and in this place it is no small item. I figured a little in the columns of of the paper as I become more bold I branch out some.

*Wednesday 24* — Went up to Saratoga and returned in time for dinner. Afternoon figured some and stoped at Cooks store to give him time to do out door business. Evening spent in writing.

*Thursday 25* — Remained in Omaha until the Mail arrived and was distributed. Accepted an invitation to ride up to Saratoga. Dined at Mr. Smileys one of our Saratoga neighbors. Found my tenants moving out of the office. Set the Painters at work. Spent the afternoon with two neighbors Mr. Gant and Mr Smiley in Surveying a whole block which I am trying to get by changing off other lots. An entire block is small enough for *my residence*.

*Friday 26* — By previous engagement went out to see a claim belonging to "Dick Darling." He made his claim in Sept. 1854, being still under age he cannot preempt it. Has sold off 160 acres last year. Has talked so much with me about it I agreed to go out and see it.

Dick Darling, the only name I know for the person, Came here before a house, except the "big six" was erected. He resides in town in a very small cabin, the only one standing of the first cabins built here. Lives alone and has done for three years in the same cabin. He has got some property has owned largely here but sold when he got a fair advance. When he first came to the place he went up to Saratoga staked out 160 acres one after noon came down and sold his claim for five dollars. The man who bought the claim sold in a short time for twenty-five dollars. Although Dick is under 21 years of age he is considered one of the first pioneers and allowed to vote. Is a general favorite but too much like boys who do not appretiate money. He thinks he can speculate when he gets short and make his expenses. Does nothing and spend his money extravigantly. Is here two or three times a day when in town. So much for *Dick Darling*.

The Claim we were to see is six miles west by the section lines. The route we were obliged to go makes the distance traveled eight or ten miles. Six miles west by the traveled road we come to one of the smaller Papillion creeks. A late freshet had carried away the bridge so that teams could not cross. We took the horse from the buggy and led him across on a plank. Then took the buggy down the bank by main strength and crossed that likewise on a plank. Three miles more and we reached one of the Main Papillons or as it is more commonly called the "*little Pappio*." The claim was immediately on the west side of the creek. For the last half mile we had left the road reaching the creek opposite the claim some three miles nearer than by the road. We took the harness from the horse and hitched him where he could feed while we were riconnoitring. The logg over which Dick was in the habit of crossing had been carried away leaving us in a dillema about how we should cross. From the top of an Elm which hung over the stream suspended a grape vine. Dick went up this vine to the top of the elm and down the elm which grew on the opposite side thus landing safely. Not being myself a climer I concluded to try the stream. According stripped and swam across which was easy enough the distance only being about twenty feet. I found the claim much more valuable than I had supposed. I am trying to make a trade for it if I do I shall preempt it for my own use it is not too far from Omaha to suit me. On the Claim is a small grove a number of springs and a stone quarry. Through said claim runs the Papillion at the east end. And lengthwise running East is the first stream I have seen in the west with stone bottom. The stream is like our eastern streams clear and rapid. Tumbling along over rocks and pebbles. I was charmed delighted with the place and it was difficult for me to refrain from expressing my admiration as I was looking with a view of purchasing I kept silent. The place has advantages but one or two know of in fact it has never been examined except from a distance and only by two or three. We found Indian devices carved in the rock and on the margin of the stream were otter and wild turky track in great numbers. If I succeed in getting hold of the claim I will make a thorough examination and report at length.

Steamers to day New Monongehola, Omaha and Watassa.

*Saturday, 27* — Another week is ended, and my mind is away east with my family where I long to be in person or to have them with me here in the West. It is a long time to look forward to the earliest day we may be together again at best. I look upon it all for the best be the result whatever it May.

A threatening rain prevented my going to Saratoga this morning as I had intended. The storm however did not commence until about noon. Kept up the most of the afternoon. It has now nearly cleared up and is delightful in the extreme. The air cool and refreshing making it one of the best of nights to sleep. It is early but the house being so very still I will retire. The family were out to a dance last evening, except Myself.

The "Edenburgh" and "Wattassa" are in today. Although quite wakefull and lonely I will say *good night* and go to bed.

*Sunday 28.* — A clear pleasant atmosphere tempted me to take one of my accostomed strolls. Went up to the Deacons and found him ready to accompany me as soon as he should get his breakfast. He had partially agreed to go up the Night previous and stop over to Mr Griffins and come down with them after dinner to church. Mr Griffins farm is about three miles west of Omaha, very pleasantly situated on the high and rolling prarie, and like all the prarie of Nebraska beautiful beyond description. We had a delightful walk. Found the family a very agreeable one, consisting of Mr and Mrs Griffin two sons and two Daughters the oldest a boy near fourteen. Go wherever you will among Nebraska pioneers and you will find intelligence and refinement equal to the eastern states and Mr Griffins family was no exception. They seemed much pleased with our visit as they have few neighbors. Our dinner was a grand one the three most important articles in the bill of fare, to suit my taste, was Strawberries and cream, green peas and dutch cheese. Mr. G. Has some 340 acres of land ten of which is timber all paid for and not a foot of waste land in the lot. In five years it will be as great a fortune as any man wants or at least ought to have. I got some Ideas about how to manage my farm.

Soon after reaching Mr. G's I notice the children coughed a good deal. I made bold to enquire the cause which was answered thus. "Lutherra, the oldest girl about eleven went down to Omaha to get subscribers for the "Casket" and "Home" and brought back a club of sufficient to entitle her to a premium, and also brought home the Measles which the last ones that had it was just recovering from. Here on the wild praries of Nebraska I found the "Home" and "Casket," farther west than I expected to find it. They were pleased to learn I was the Mr Beadle whose name was on the books.

At about three o'clock P. M. after the pleasantest kind of a time with a pleasant family we left with the family who came down to church in their double waggon. Again I must say I cannot make it seem to me that this is a new county but about three years since the first settlement was commenced in the Territory.

At our levee we found the steamer "Council Bluffs" on our return.

*Monday 29* — Remained at Omaha during the forenoon expecting important letters. After dinner went up to Saratoga where I found a number of persons wanting lots Who were on hand with lumber to commence building. The family occupying My office had got into a house of their own. And the office was occupied by a Mr Keller and Mr. Gray who were keeping Bachelors hall while they are erecting their buildings. Gray & Keller came on with Mr Tuttles party. They are from Little Falls N. Y. Steamer "Alonzo Childs" in.

*Tuesday 30* — Immediately after breakfast went up to Saratoga. Had a Meeting of the company at the Central House. I was solicited to take the office of Post Master in Saratoga, but declined for reasons just and sensible. The furniture for the "Central house" came yesterday on the Steamer "Alonzo Childs" and is being arranged in the House preparitory to the arrival of the landlord who is expected about the 4th July. The Companys meeting adjourned to meet tomorrow over to the Bluffs. Returned to Omaha after donating two lots. Found a letter under date of June 15th from wife and daughter also one from Mr Warner who had arrived home safe but very much exhausted. The Steamer E. A. "Ogden" in.

*Wednesday July 1.* — Spent this day at Council Bluffs in a meeting of the S. S. L. Co. Returned between five and six P. M. Found my friend S. M. Hall in town also John L. Beadle who is now making his home at Bellevue. He is a very pleasant man, is a decendant from the same parent stock some over one hundred years back to distant however to claim a relationship. His Great-grandfather and my Grandfather were probably Cousins. The Estabrook family have gone this evening to an Episcopal fair. My inclinations are not in that directions.

*Thursday 2* — Went to Saratoga, rode up with General Estabrooks family and the Hon. Judge Black who were going to Fleronce. From the Generals we drove up to "Pioneer block" where we took in the Judge. Were obliged to wait for the general to transact some business. Our position was directly in front of Armstrong & Clarks' store at which place was Miss Clark standing in the door of the store. This was the first time I had a fair view of Miss Clark by daylight, and the more I saw of her the more I thought I saw a resemblance to my wife.

At Saratoga spent most of the day with a Mr. Patrick one of the Executive Committee. Mr Patrick was presented last evening with a son. The first child born in Saratoga. He is entitled to a corner lot. The Steamer "Minne-ha-ha" is in this evening.

*Friday 3,* — Remained in Omaha until Middle afternoon transacting business with Mr. Hall then rode up to Saratoga with Mr. Tuttle and some men from Pittsburgh who are going to build largely in Saratoga. At Saratoga we found the Central house aranged for a dance which was to come off this evening being the commencing exercises for the 4th. Returned to Omaha with Mr Hall who had come up with his team, in time for a late supper.

About nine O'clock, Judge Black and Myself took the Generals horse and buggy and rode up to the "Central House" Saratoga to the dance. Found the Dancing hall filled to the utmost of its capacity. Council Bluffs, Iowa Floronce, Omaha, Plattsmouth and Bellview in this territory were all represented comprising the elite of Nebraska. And I doubt if a more refined or intelligent assemblage could be got together in any of the eastern cities. Judge Black participated in the dance and became generally acquainted. While I, notwithstanding the urgent solicitations of my very few acquaintance remained

"An idle looker on in Venice"

satisfied to make up my enjoyment of the evening in beholding others enjoyment and feasting from a distance on the attraction of Miss Clark, who on a *close* view did not bear the happy resemblance to my wife she did when distant the length of the Hall.

Soon after Supper a recess was taken in order to sweep the dancing floor and we were obliged to occupy three of the reception rooms bringing us into close quarters. Judge Black introduced me to several ladies during the recess one of which, and the only one whose name I remember was Miss Dora Clark, the youngest sister of three Miss Clarks in attendance, the oldest one being the person who so much resembles my wife. An introduction to a few of the ladies and the exhilerating effect of the supper, and trimmings, made the balance of the evening pass off equally as agreeable as the first. I did not however make the acquaintance of *the* Miss Clark. Between two and three o'clock The Judge and myself left the balance of the company to their own enjoyment and returned home.

*Saturday, 4.* — Got up to breakfast about 8 o'clock. The day was ushered in as usual in the East by fireing a salute and ringing bells. A military company came over from the Bluffs and Joined in our celebration. Which was got up and went through with in the usual manner of such things. The oration was delivered by Judg Black in "Park Wild" Grove. Every body "and the rest of mankind was there." The oration was extempore, and although the Judge is one of the best speakers, an occurance took place which very much marred the whole proceedings. Respect to parties concerned prevents my placing on record the facts. Miss Clark was at the celebration and recognized by Mr. Tuttle as bearing a striking resemblance to my wife. So it cannot be attributed to her personal charms, sufficient to make my wife jealous if she *does* resemble her. After the celebration was over the streets were filled with men who began to feel the effects to too much strong drink. It is the besetting sin of Omaha in fact all places on the river are notorious for habits of intemperance, and the young men are coming up with very immoral habits. Money is made easy and is spent freely.

After tea I took a stroll up on Capital hill and went on the top of the Capitol which is approaching completion. Will be ready for the roof in a few days. The Steamer "Ben Bolt" came in this evening.

*Sunday, 5.* — This has been a very warm day and I have had but little time to write, been quite busy in taking care of Judg Black who is not well today and has required considerable attention.

*Monday morning, July 6* — My attention being so much occupied with the Judge I have had time only to write a few lines in my diary. Probably can write some this evening. He is much better this morning. Must go up to Saratoga directly after breakfast. E. F BEADLE

*Monday Evening 6.* — Spent the most of the day at Saratoga returning found the Judg nearly well. The steamer "Emma" came in and passed up.

*Tuesday, 7* — Donated a large number of lots in Saratoga. We now have about fifty houses in town ready for occupation and they are occupied too. Wrote a number of letters this afternoon to Eastern parties. Among the number was one to Mr Turner also to G. B. Rich.

*Wednesday, 8* — Immediately after Breakfast walked up to Saratoga with a gentleman from Pittsburgh Pa, who has six houses for Saratoga 16 X 32 feet two story high. Selected lots for him and returned to Omaha at one o'clock P. M. having been on foot all the forenoon. Received a letter from Robert Adams, and a protest on one of the notes Mr. Wowzer gave me. Wrote a half dozen letters.

Toward tea time the Steamer "Moses Greenwood" came in freighted mostly for Saratoga. Went down found Mr Killen the Pittsburgh man there. His buildings and Men to put them up was on board the "Greenwood". Having but little loading to put off at Omaha, I had no time to return for my supper and still go up on the boat to Saratoga. Accordingly I took tea aboard. The Saratoga landing is but a mile or less above the Omaha landing. The captain says the Saratoga landing is as good as any on the river. He further says a bar is forming front of Omaha and in a year or two all boats must land at Saratoga with the Omaha freight. The Captain was delighted with the place. After tea we went up on the table land by Pacific Avenue where we had a fine view of the town and the improvements. We then went to the Springs where a demijohn from the boat was filled with water from the Sulphur springs. The party that went up to the spring was about twenty in number, including Captain Thomas, crew and passengers. All expressed themselves delighted with what they saw and will speak of Saratoga as it is, among their craft.

The "Moses Greenwood" is the second steamer that ever landed at Saratoga, and the first one to break the stillness of the atmosphere by her steam whistle. She went through all the preliminary signals and *et ceteras* of landing at a large city. I claim to be the first person of the Sulphur Springs Land Co. that ever landed from a steamer at Saratoga. The freight of the "Moses Greenwood" was mostly lumber and building materials. She discharged forty-one thousand feet of lumber, forty-two thousand shingles, and doors windows and hardware to match. Did not get all off untill eleven o'clock, but the moon was in its full and it was a delightfull evening and the time passed rapidly. During which *I* gassed *some*. Judg Black left on the Moses Greenwood who stoped only about an hour at the city of Omaha.

*Thursday 9* — Four months this morning since I left for this place. Got up this morning before the sun and wrote. Among the peculiarities of the climate of this country over the East where I have resided is this, notwithstanding we have hotter weather here, there always is a breeze during the day to rarify the atmosphere and the evenings are cool and delightful beyond description, and one can sleep comfortable under a sheet and light quilt, awaking in the morning completely refreshed and invigorated. On the contrary in the east during the months of July and August the nights are as hot as the days, and one gets up in the morning Completely exhausted. This I consider a great advantage but is small compared to some of the *Natural* advantages of this *Great Country* west of the "big Muddy." *We* find the Steamer Admiral in this Morning.

After breakfast went up as usual to Saratoga. Called on Mr Tuttle and The Zollars who are occupying Mr Tuttles house. The old Izard place built and occupied first by Governor Izard. Tuttle calls the place "Grandmother Izards." Stopped and gassed some with Tuttle. The steamboat landing last evening at Saratoga and what the Captain said set us to gasing some.

Returning from Saratoga at noon found a letter from Brother Frank which was very interesting to me. Figured during most of the afternoon with our Pittsburgh man and succeeded in making a trade that pleased me. Wrote to Frank and spent the evening with Cook. Thus this day closed. In addition to the "Admiral" we have at the landing The Steamers "Col. Crossman" and The "Watossa." How soon, if ever, is a wonderment to me, that I shall be watching the arrivals of the steamers to see My family.

*Friday 10* — Got a very early breakfast, and went up to Mr. Tuttles where the Zollars live and made arangements to go with them to look at Dick Darlings and other claims. They to come up to Saratoga after me should they get ready in time. Went around examining the Saratoga improvements and staked out for the foundation of another house reaching my office about noon. In half hours time the Zollers came, three of them. Had a basket of bread meat fried cakes pies and Mohawk butter and cheese, for our dinner. As soon as we despatched the dinner. We started in a south west direction across the prarie. On reaching the first papillion creek where it was necessary to take the horse from the waggon to cross we discovered we were going in the direction of a thunder storm which threatened to be a severe one, and would so wet evry thing as to be unpleasant tramping in the tall grass after we should reach the claim. We accordingly decided to abandon the trip and come again some other day. The rain overtook us before we reached Omaha but as each buggy had an umbrella we were very well protected, the greater part of the storm going west.

At the generals I found judge Furguson and his wife from Belleview. The came up to court which was adjourned. In the evening B. P. Rankin another candidate for Congress in opposition to General Estabrook, addressed the citizens of Omaha. The Gen. being up country could not reply to Mr. R. as we all thought it would be necessary, As Mr R has the impudence of a highway man and will state falsehood as quick as the truth. A letter had been received at the office for the General from one of his friends at Nebraska City. Mrs E opened it and we all read it the judge said it must be read at Rankins meeting. The substance of the letter was that there had been a very large political meeting at Nebraska City, in which a Mr Mickles Bennett and Rankin tried to have all their own way, got up resolutions pledging the County to go for Rankin, the resolutions were debated four hours and then *lost 4 to 1*. Mr Rankin took occasion in his speech in Nebraska City to denounce Omaha and the Ferry Company. Said "great injustice had been done Nebraska City by Omaha and the Ferry Co and he Mr. R. had always been opposed to Omaha and its interest." I took this letter to a Mr Chippman, late Judge, who said if occasion required he would read it at the meeting. Feeling a strong interest in the matter Judge Furguson and Myself went up to the meeting. I never heard such a braging speech, he said "the whole north and south was going for him, he was a *tower of strength*. At Nebrask City he had the strongest assurance. He produced a letter purpoting to be written by Mr Muckles and addressed to Dr. Miller of this place. The letter set fourth the pledges of the meeting for Rankin and mentioned that resolutions had been passed. Mr R. then read the resolutions which he had and stated they were adopted almost unanimous, on this subject he dwelt largely. "He should carry all before him South of the Platt." And now he was going to work North of the Platt. Closed his speech by appealing to Omaha and its interest which he *had always advocated*.

Mr. Chippman was called for by men in the secret. Asked Mr

Rankin to allow him the privilege of reading another letter that had been received and would throw still more light on the subject of the meeting at Nebraska City. Mr R. Concented after Knowing who was the writer of the letter and to whom it was addressed. Mr Chipman then got up and in the most cool and deliberate manner read the letter. Mr R. Interrupted him a number of times to know who was meant as being opposed to Omaha &c. Mr Chippman then went back read slow emphasising every word and then said yes it is you it, it, *means you.* I never saw a man so taken, down it gave the lie to all Mr. Rankins bombast and Mr R. did not try to deny it. Mr. R lost votes at that meeting if he has any here to loose which I doubt.

The storm continued during the evening so that the Judge and his wife stoped with us at the generals. After gloryfying over the meeting a short time we retired at midnight.

*Saturday 11* — Got up at four o'clock. Made a fire then called Mrs. Estabrook, and surprised the Judge and his wife with a breakfast as they must start at five. Judge F. is one of the best men we have in the territory.

The reason for my getting up to build the fire this morning was, The hired man and his wife was out on their claim preparing to pre-empt, leaving Me the Man of the house. This mornings mail brought me a letter from my wife, which I immediately answered. After dinner walked up to one of the Pittsburgh houses which is being erected on the south line of Saratoga. Returned in time to save a wet Jacket. Lay down and took a sleep, the first time in the afternoon. We having the best of weather. Rain just about often enough. Crops never looked better any where. One can raise enough here off of a farm the size of Brother Bams in one season to support one five years, and do it easier than a single crop can be raised in the town of Franklin.

Br. Cook has his house completed except lathing and plastering which he does not intend to do until fall, has got a stove and every thing is ready for Lib.

Spent this evening writing directions for Mr. Gridly, who is going to Buffalo in the morning, and will see the Turners and perhaps make a trade with them.

Between daylight and dark took a walk up town past Mr. Clarks. The young ladies were out front of the door but it was to dark to distinguish them. Steamer "New Monongahala" in to day.

*Sunday 12* — After breakfast took a walk up to Saratoga to get my washing which is done there. Cook has not been up before since the first sermon was preached there. The change seemed wonderfull to him. He says he thinks my chances are far ahead of his. It may be so but I should like a little of the results of what the future seemes to be at the *present* time. One advantage Cook has over me is the fact he has a house ready to go into and his family has the money to come out here with and probably soon be here. When we got back from Saratoga found the folks to church. I took a good supply of rain water and went to my room where I had a glorious wash, then comenced writing.

There is now a pleanty of places where I could get my board at Saratoga, but I could not get as good accomodations. I now have a room to myself and every thing I could ask for and if I should be sick I should have the best of care. I am well acquanted with The Generals family and feel at home and do not wish to change for an uncertainty. At any other place I should be obliged to share my bed with every body and three or four beds in a room and all sorts of people for associates. The Generals family are plan every day sort of people, although intelligent and educated and their associates are the best in the Territory including the dignitary and territorial officials. I could not have got another such a place to board in this entire teritory. Were I sick at most places I should be neglected or hustled off to the pest house. I shall ever feel under lasting obligations to General Estabroks family. Mrs. E. Is none of your *hitytity flyaways* but a substantial matter-of-fact woman. And is quite a business woman. One whose acquaintance is worth cultivating and the better you know her the better you like her. She is a large woman almost masculine. Never fretts or gets out of patience with her children. Is always the same decided, firm, calculating, and patient woman, ever sensative to the wants and sympathies of those around her, whether in her own house or that of her neigbors. Such is my hostess. The description of whome has served to fill this page that I may send it with letters by Mr Gridly and thereby save time.

Closing up my package of letters I took them up to Mr. Kellums and delivered to Mr Gridley. He goes over to Council Bluffs in the omnibuss this afternoon and startes across the county in the Stage at 2 o'clock in the morning. He expects to be with his family as soon as next Saturday. I almost envied him his happiness and it made me quite homesick like to bid him goodby. He has got himself fairly established here in a Banking house and is doing well. Is delighted with the country. Was on the old fogy order when he came here and I did not suppose *he* would like here. He is however strongly attached to the place. Goes east to arrange business and will return the fore part of September.

The steamer "Dan Converse" came in this morning about daylight.

*Monday 13*  Went early to Saratoga. Spent a very busy day. Returned on foot about two o'clock P. M. and immediately got into a waggon and rode up and back again. Figured some and made a good day of it.

*Tuesday 14*  A threatning storm prevented my going to Saratoga this morning. Spent the time in writing letters. Afternoon went up and examined improvements. Stoped at Mr Smileys and made arangements with Miss Smiley for my children to go to school.

*Wednesday 15* — The hotest day I ever knew. Still the constant breeze makes it very comfortable when compared with the hot days in New York where the is no breeze. The themometer has ranged to 100 most of the day in the shade. I have walked to Saratoga and back. Then rode up and back. Selected a lot for a Union church which is soon to be erected. Received and answered a letter from Br. Frank. The Steamers "Asa Wilgus" and "Alonzo Childs" in today.

*Thursday 16* — A threatning storm prevented my going to Saratoga this morning. In the afternoon stoped in the store for Cook under pay of course. Equally hot today with less air stiring than any day since I have been in Nebraska. We have had an election to day to decide whether this County will take $200,000 stock in M. & M. R R. to be expended on the west end of the route terminating a Council Bluffs. This city polled 1156 votes. This vote showes we must have at least a population of $3000 including Saratoga which has near 100 voters at this time.

The vote was favorable to taking the stock by a large majority. Florance voted largely against it. In fact they would burn their own town if they could spite Omaha. Almost every town in the territory seems to be jealous of Omaha and oppose every thing favorable to Omaha. The result has a tendency to build up Omaha instead of the reverse as they would wish. The steamers in today are the "Edenburg" "Dan Converse" and "Watossa." Wrote a letter this afternoon to Frankford Mower Co. Minnesota.

*Friday 17* — Guns firing all the morning over the result of the R. R Election. Excessively warm. Not feeling will I attend store for Mr Cook this forenoon and wrote a number of letters. Received a letter from wife and answered the same hour. Also received advises of the shipment of my goods stating I ought to receive them as early as the 25th of July. I shall not look for them before the 10th of August.

Four o'clock in the afternoon rode up to Saratoga with a Lutheran clergyman who wished to select a lot for a church. Made a number of selections to submit to the Company. The Steamer Omaha Just in.

*Saturday — 18.* Walked up early to Saratoga with Dick Darling, to show lots I wished to trade for his claim, have not succeeded in tradeing and probably shall not. The price asked for the claim is $800. At the price claims are held here I consider it cheap and should buy it but cannot unless I dicker. Spent the afternoon and evening with the Secretary of the Saratoga Compy. Give him my bill for cervises rendered upt to Monday next, and the terms I would continue work upon. We have a Meeting on Monday and I shall then know if I am to be paid and if so how much, and if not paid, I shall devote no time to the company, but make different arrangments as to what I shall do to keep off starve-to-death.

*Sunday, 19.* After breakfast walked up to Cooks. Found him ready for a stroll, which we both improved. The weather being cloudy made it a treat when compared with the previous hot days when the thermometer ranged at 100. We walked about three miles down the river along the edge of the bluff returning come up the bottom along the margin of the river. It was a region of country I have never before visited and was delighted with it as only this territory can delighe one. Found some fine raspberries.

Afternoon clear and hot. Wrote some, slept some, and fretted some. In the evening took a walk. Steamer "E. A. Ogden up from St. Louis.

*Monday, 20* — Went up early to Saratoga and prepared my report for the meeting to take place at Eleven o'clock. After the meeting had convend I submitted my report, which was satisfactory. Then left my bill for my time and resignation with Secretary to submit to the Company and left for Omaha. Here I found a letter from Robert Adams from which I am lead to think Frank has accepted my proposition on the Wisconsin land, if so I shall look for my family within a week unless I hear to the contrary. My resignation was accepted and the payment for services deferred one week. A long talk with Mr. Tuttle this evening resulted. Just as I wished.

*Tuesday 21* — Walked up to Saratoga and delivered the papers to my succcsor and immediately returned. Contracted to sell the lot and office belonging to Mr. Cacket for $500. Received as the first installment $115. Stoped at the stove store in the afternoon.

The letter received from Robert yesterday under date of the 9th set me to figuring and I came to the conclusion I should look for my family the last of this week provided I did not hear from them to the contrary. Just at Dusk we saw the Steamer "Minnehaha" coming up the river. Cook and Myself figured up the time again and decided it was barely possible either of our families might be on board. So down we went to the levee. I for the first to look for my family. Slight as the chances were, the possibilluty was sufficient to excite us some what. We were the first on the boat as she touched the shore. Not finding our friends we joked each other some. Went up town. Took some ice cream and retired.

*Wednesday 22* — Stoped this day in the store for Mr. Cook. Being few costomers in passed the time in reading and writing. Received letters from Mitler Orton & Co and Cousin Benjamin of Tenessee. Watched anxious for the morning mail in the hope of hearing from Frank or wife.

Nothing being received I am lead to look, still with more assurance for the arrival of my family.

*Thursday 23* — Remained in the store during the forenoon. No letter from Cooperstown. Going to dinner heard the whistle of a steamer. Hurried to landing, found it was the new ferry "Omaha City" for this place built at Pittsburgh Pa. The Admiral now due was expected every hour. I though perhaps my family would be on board, and left directions with Mrs. Estabrook, and after dinner went out to Dick Darlings and others claims, in company with the Mr. Zollars. Had a very pleasant time concidering I was suffering with a boil the first one I ever recollect of having. We did not return until about nine o'clock. I was somewhat anxious to know if the Steamer Admiral was in and if so had my family Come? Before reaching the Generals I discovered no boat had arrived and of course my family could not be here. I was not disappointed as the grounds on which I base my reasons for looking for my family are not the more substantial.

*Friday – 24* — Passed a sleepless night so severe was the pain of my Boil. It is located on my backbone between my hips. I think it is a blood boil. Those that have been thus afflicted with Jobs Comforters alone can appretiate the affliction. I did not sleep untile after daylight and then so sound was my sleep I was called twice to breakfast and heard nothing of it. The Steamer "Watossa" from St. Joseph came in during the time and fired an arrival gun still it did not awake me. As soon however as my boil commenced paining me again I awoke and was in time for my breakfast but surprised to learn the above facts.

*Evening* Oh such a day I have passed and such agony as I am in. At noon I was obliged to leave the store, since which time I have been unable to sit, walk, stand or lay, been in every possble position only for a moment at a time. How anxiously I have watched for the Admiral hoping my family Might be on board. I am well cared for here but what a blessing would be the kind hand of a wife to aid in soothing my pains or give me her heartfelt sympathies, and my little children to come around me and express their unaffected sorrow. It seemes I could bear my pains with much more fortitude.

I cannot write now. I will have a large poltice made and take a dose of perrigoric or lodnum and try to so stupify myself as to get some rest. Good night.

*Saurday and Sunday, 25th and 26* — The poltice releived my pain the whole night, but the opiate I had taken made me wakefull instead of sleepy and I did not close my eyes to sleep until daylight. Kept my bed and room all day Saturday except when the mail come in went up and got a paper from Irwin Mailed the 15th. This satisfies me that Frank might have been in receipt of my letter eight days and still write an answer which I should now have. This fact streangthens my convictions that my family are on the way to this place. Could not write any this day being in constant pain and two nights without sleep. My nerves had become completely unstrung. At seven in the evening my pain stoped and such a relief I never before experienced. On going to bed renewed the potice which renewed the pain also. Bore it until midnight then removed it and found the boil was discharging some. Dressed myself and walked the room about an hour during a storm. Lopped down on the floor and got a good sleep. Crawled on the bed with my cloths on and forgot my troubles until morning. On waking heard a steamer puffing. Hobbled down to the boat which was the "Col. Crosman." As she came nearer and nearer we saw plenty of children that might be Irwin and Sophia but the ladies all had children in arms. They could not be mate. Cook was down before the boat got in not to look for Lib as he has a letter stating she will not start yet awhile. But equally anxious with me to see my family. We did not have the pleasure however. The Steamers "Emma" and "Admiral" are hourly expected. They may be here before night. It is now about ten o'clock A. M. Sunday and I am feeling quite comfortable. My boil has undoubtedly had its ache out. I am however about used up myself.

*Evening* Been up to Cooks for the last hour chatting. Came home in the rain. The day has been warm and showery. This evening is cooler and there is a slow rain set in which seemes it would continue all night. I have had a very comfortable day of it. My boil continueing to discharge every few minutes. No further information from boats from St. Louis. Now for a good nights rest free from pain.

*Monday 27* — A dilghtful day, rested well last night. Have been busy attending to my boil. Sent to Saratoga for my wash which I had left at a Mr Grey's the man from Little Falls. He had been so carefull as to put the clothes in his trunk, and having occasion to go out to preempt took his Trunk with him and cosequently my clothes so I am shirtless for a few days a sad misshap when one has a boil discharging freely on his back.

No letters still from wife or Frank. Have one under date of the 18th from James Crocker in reply to one written a week or more after the one I wrote Frank. I am getting anxious to know his decission and to be relieved of the anxiety with which I am watching the arrival of Steamers for my family. The Steamer Admiral arrived this Evening. Left St. Louis the 17th. Had a number of Lady passengers and Some children. Could not pick out my wife and children in the crowd.

A Letter from Mrs Cook received by the Deacon today informs him as a reason for here not coming as requested she had been and was very sick then but fearing to give Cook unnecessary uneasiness she did not say the worst. But made various excuses about the warm weather &c.

Propositions have been made to me to day I will not mention at present.

*Tuesday, 28* — Received a letter this morning from Mr. Cockett, from which I learn that my wife and children are still in Cooperstown. This fact together with one other probably decides that I shall not see my family here very soon. The proposition I wrote of yesterday cannot be accepted or executed on account of my wife's not being in the territory. Particulars I will give at another time.

It is quite provoking to me to have Frank delay answering my letter so long as he has. He may have a reasonable excuse. I cannot however conceive its nature if he has any excuse to offer. I wrote him today.

Walked up to Saratoga and back this afternoon. Found many new improvements going on. The Landlord for the "Central House" had arrived and was aranging the furniture and carpets. Has his help all with him, will open the first of next week. Has a number of rooms engaged already. Is to run his omnibus regular to Omaha, fare a dime a head.

This evening had a talk with Dick Darling. He says he will accept one of my previous propositions for his claim. I think I shall arrange matters with him and go out at once and pre-empt.

Received pay for my cervices for the company this morning and paid assessments on three shares and settled up my board bill.

*Wednesday, 29* — Received letters this forenoon from wife and Brother Frank. It appears Frank has written me a letter I have not received, which has caused all this anxiety I have felt, and been the cause I expecting my family when they were still in Cooperstown with no thought of even starting. I have no doubt all will be for the best. I think so at least.

Closed my bargain with Dick Darling this morning and passed papers. We are making preparations to go out in the morning to live on it five days and then prove up and preempt. Expect a happy time among the musketoes.

Answered letters this afternoon and in the evening went up to Mr Tuttles and had a chatt with him. It is now bed time and I will retire. Tomorrow night expect to sleep out at the farm. Good Night.
At the Generals ten o'clock at night.
July 29th 1857
E. F. Beadle

*Rock Brook Farm Six Miles West of Omaha July 31, 1857.*
On the Big Pappio Creek and Nin-na-bak. In township 15 range 12 East section 28. North half of South East quarter, and East half of South West quarter.

*Two o'clock P. M.* Our cabin being finished, preliminarries aranged for an actual residence and having had a short nap after lunch I will commence to bring down my diary to date:—

*July 30, 1857* — Immediately after breakfast Set about collecting suplies for "the farm." Borrowed a Sheet-iron cook stove of the deacon, an old coffee pot, plates, cups and saucers, knives and forks, pepper, salt, flour and a little butter of Mrs. Estabrook. Bought a fourteen pound chunck of dried beef 7 lbs. crackers, 4 loaves bread, 4 lbs. sugar one quarter tea and four pound nails. These we packed into a tea chest adding the contents of Mrs. E's cake box. Next we supplied ourselves with two blankets and two Buffalo robes, Hickory shirts, the poorest pair of pants we had, a revolver a bowe knife and fowling piece. Stowed all into the lumber waggon of the Generals and with his man Jake for driver started via Saratoga. Thermometer at 100. At Saratoga we took in some dozen pine boards for roof to cabin and a glazed window sash, also two bottles Turners blackbury Brandy. For the information of my temperance friends I would state that this brandy is not intoxicating. Is used more as a cordial or for medicinal purposes.

Leaving Saratoga we struck across the prarie intersecting the Elkhorn road some two miles from Omaha. At the first Pappio we succeeded in crossing without unloading which we did not expect when we started. Two miles more across the prarie brought us to the big Pappi opposite the farm or claim. Here Mr. Darling, who is to be my witness forded the stream and fell three trees across the creek all together, forming a fine crossing. In a half hours time we had our lumber packed across and landed on the South side of the Pappio together with our supplies. Our Man Jake returned with his team, Darling and myself commenced packing our effects over to the cabin a distance of one fourth of a mile. Two packloads each and we sat down and took our dinner and supper together. After this we had five packloads each before our lumber was all on the ground. Now came the putting up of the shanty or Cabin the one previously erected by Darling never had a roof, and had consequently blown down. We worked like men to get up our cabin as the muttering Thunder and heavy black clouds at the south and west threatened a storm, which would make a shelter comfortable. It was sundown however before the roof was on our cabin. This being completed we crossed the little brook to where some German people had been making hay on my claim and took the liberty of taking what we could carry. This we aranged in one corner of the cabin and sprad thereon our robes and blankets and straightened ourselves out to sleep two as tired men as ever saw the sun go down. To prevent sickness from drinking an excess of water we tried a little of the Blackbury juice.

The storm continued threatening with tremendous thunder and vivid lightning. It passed arround to the south-west not more than a dozzen drops falling on our cabin.

During the night we had a constant Seranade. So that we could not sleep. The numbers of the troop were countless. Their music was very romantic and extremely fine toned, but the multitude of the performers made the whole air vocal for miles around. At first we were delighted with such sweet music to sleep by, and all would have passed off pleasantly. Had not our Seranade troop become to affectionate, and were determined every one of them to salute us with a Kiss before they would allow us to go to sleep. We allowed a few to try it by way of experiment but they kissed so warmly the effect was painfull for a half hour after, and we determined to fight them off which could only be done by "smoking them out," and it was near daylight in the morning before we could sleep, at all.

*Friday 31* — Our Serenaders left us about daylight and we improved the time until 8 o'clock in sleep when we got up so weak we could hardly stand. Put up our stove and made a fire. Cooked a little dried beef and made some tea in a large basin, our coffee pot we found leaked. Laid our window sash on the tea chest for a table and took a hearty breakfast our tea tasting fine. After breakfast walked over to see our German friends who were cutting our hay. Mowed a little for exercise. The company making hay consisted of two men and one woman. The woman used the cythe just as well as the men.

Leaving the hay makers I started of to find the limits of the farm. At the South East corner I was met by the German woman of the hay-field who came up to see that I was not going to claim a portion of her farm. I satisfied her all was right. She invited me to her cabin which was but a quarter of a mile South, her land joining mine. I went with her but declined going in. Went to the spring and got a drink and borrowing a spade started off to find other corners and mark them. Returned to my Cabin at noon. Took a bath in the creek, a lunch, a snoose and the commenced writing While Dick Darling mowed some grass to enlarge our bed. Dug out the spring and commenced ditching for a drain from the spring.

During the afternoon the German woman came to our spring for water for the men making hay. She agreed to sell us some milk at night if we would come for it to the cabin.

About four o'clock it commenced as it did yesterday afternoon clouding up and Thundering. The wind blew severely making our cabin tremble. It rained on all sides of us but not sufficient here to test the utility of our rooff which we fear will serve as a poor protection during a rain-storm. At half past seven we concluded it would not rain here, so we took each a loaf of bread and spoon and started for our German neighbor when we each disposed of a quart of new milk, sitting out doors with a barrell head for a table. Coming home we saw some splendid sights in the way of lightning which performed such freaks as I never before saw.

*Saturdaay Aug. 1, 1857* — Another night of torments from our Serenaders has just passed still we managed to get more sleep than the previous night, much to the gratification of our tormenters who covered the walls of our cabin when daylight came gorged with our best blood, giving the cabin the appearance of being ornimented with red beads.

Another trial as cook succeeded most admirably and we had a fine breakfast of dried beef with thickned gravy bread, crackers, cake and tea. Dishes being washed Darling went to work on the ditch while I resumed my writing.

Three years ago this day Dick Darling first saw this claim. At the time there was but one house in Omaha and much of the time for a few weeks he was the only white man this side of the Missourie river among the Indians then more pleanty than the white men are now. He came out here from Omaha alone to see the country. Traveled all along the Pappio and fixed upon this spot as being the most desireable and lovely any where in this reagion and determined to be the possessor at some future day if in his power. On or about the 24th September following Darling and a companion came out and marked the limits of his claim including all the most valuable portion comprising near

600 acres. Since the government surveys were made, last summer, he has given 80 acres to one man sold 160 to another and 40 to a third in order to piece out each ones claim, he having more than he could hold. The original claim was made sufficiently large to be sure to comprise in one claim, when surveyed, all that most valuable portion. The claim I have purchased comprises three Eighties 240 acres. I can only pre-empt 160 this however includes all the timber and rock the remaining 80 is bare prarie with the Min-na bah running through it. It is preempted on all sides and there is no danger of its being jumped. I shall hold it by claim club, improving that part, and as soon as the land comes in market cover it with an 80 acre land warrant. Thus securing 240 acres for the best farm in Nebraska Territory.

Three years ago the Omaha's village was about six miles below here, and the Day Darling first came out here Aug 1, 1854. The Omaha's started on their annual Buffalo hunt, passed through this claim within three rods of where our cabin now stands. The party went in indian file and were a half day in passing each Indian had a poney heavily packed which he lead by a *lorette* or lasso. The path they made is visable today and can be followed in the night. It is known as the Omaha Buffalo trail and can be followed into the heart of the Buffalo country. This trail of one summer will be visable for five years to come. Where they crossed the Min na bah is a fine gravel foot path and is in the shade of some splended elms just the place for a summer house. I shall gather some curiosities from the spot.

This morning when we first got up we saw six large Swallow tailed Eagles sitting on the dead branches of a Black walnut tree. They were a beautifull sight. Were to shy to get a shot at with a fowling piece. If we had had a rifle we would have brought one down.

Darling having worked at ditching until he was satisfied for the time, gave me up my boots he was wearing and I devoted two hours to tracing the course of the Min-na-bah and transfering it to paper just as it passes through the farm. Found otters in great plenty along the Pappio and Minnabah. Should I be here in the fall or winter I could trap enough to rig my family out in fur of the costliest kind with little trouble.

The middle and latter part of the afternoon we whiled away in our cabin reading, laughing, jokeing, story telling and snoozing. Thundered

"The Cabin I pre-empted in"

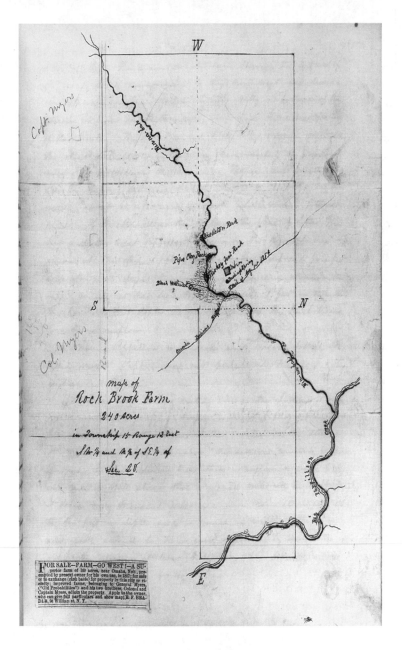

Rock Brook Farm

a little toward night but was very distant and threatened no approch in
our direction. After half past six we took our spoons and a loaf of bread
and started over to the germans to take our supper of bread and milk.
In our route we passed over the highest point on my claim if not the
highest any where in the vicinity. The prospect was grand and sublime
unlike anything I ever saw or my fancy ever imagined. In a north-west
direction the eye could follow for twenty miles the course of the Pappio
maked by the few trees that skirted its banks in every other direction as
far as the eye could see was a wide expance of rolling prarie, unmolested
by the hand of Man. It lay in silent slumber just as it was left at the
creation. No signs of human life was visible. No looing herd was seen
on the hills. No tinkling bell of the flock was herd as it wended its way
to the foald. No tired husbandman sought his cottage on the prarie.
No domestic fowl was heard to crook or cackle not even the robin or
sparrow is known here, no sound save ones own breathing is heard. The
same stillness characterises the morning, noon, and night, you rise with
the first approach of light and listen until the sun has commenced his
march in the heavens. No crowing cock saluts the morn, no rumbling
wheels or baying watch dog is heard. The same continued death like
stillness prevails as at the beginning of time. Who shall mark the change
ten years hence in this garden of the world? Enough of this.

Our German friends, (the only family in this reagion) had our milk
ready, and we were soon on our return. Stoped at an old camping ground
of the Omahas and gathered a few limbs to start our smudge to drive
of the serenaders. Darling cut a lot of grass and soon had a thick smoke
poaring up which drove off our tormenters. Enabling me to go to sleep
while Darling kept up the smudge I had the best nights rest yet.

*Sunday, 2* — Breakfast being disposed of and the dishes washed, I
gave my boots over to Darling who went to work on his ditch while I
continued my writing. An hour finished the ditch to Darling's spring a
job done worth ten dollars to the spring. Being again in the possession
of my boots I wandered in the Ninnabah exploring among the rocks
and trees, found some curious stones and a wild turkeys quill. Gathered
a lot of pipe clay took it to the cabin and manufactured a pipe in true
indian fashion, and prepared some of the clay to take east with me.

While Darling was making the ditch this morning I made a pencil sketch of the cabin which I enclose by way of illustration. I consider it a master production.

We had the promise of a visit from some of our friends in Omaha today, waited for them until three o'clock and thinking they would not come we started off for a tramp up to a Mr McCardles an Irishman living some two and a half miles up the Pappio. Followed the Indian trail to the place. Found the family enjoying themselves over their "Sod corn whiskey." The next day was to be election and the polls for this presinct was to be held at McCardles including McCardle his four sons, dick Darling and myself. It was supposed they woould poll ?o votes in some eight or ten townships. We decided to come up and vote. Returning to our cabin we found our friends had been there. Brought with them two bottles of porter which they had empted and made a good show on our provisions got out my pencil sketch. Wrote under it and posted it up in the cabin, took out my writing materials and wrote a letter calling upon us to "be at the polls the next day and look to the rural districts" "Vote for Hickneey" (one of the persons who came out) "and our names should be handed down to posterity." We regreted very much not seeing them. Consoled ourselves by going over to the Germans and finishing the last of our bread in a bowl of milk. The German walked out on my farm to show me where there is a road to pass between us running in a direct line from Chicago, a little town west of us to Omaha. Advised with him where I should have some breaking done. Also arranged with him to look after my farm and keep the fire out of the timber. All of which he will do as he has cut $100 worth of hay on my farm. The land is much better for having the grass cut as it will not burn over in the fall or spring and will yield double the amount another year He says after all the bottom land has been mowed once I can cut 150 tons of hay every season. Bottom land is so scarse here hay is a cash article. After a long walk about farming generally &c we parted and I went to the cabin when Darling had a good Smudg, so I curled down and had a good nights sleep.

*Monday 3* — Got up an hour earlier than usual. Got the breakfast ready and ate it alone Darling not wishing to get up. After breakfast prepared our cabin to leave it for Election. Our German neighbor and his man came along about eight o'clock when we armed ourselves with our revolvers and bowie knives and taking the trail in Indian file started for the polls. The Judges of election had not arrived. We here first learned we were entitled to two Constables and two justices. We accordingly nominated our German neighbor and Dick Darling at Constables and one of the McArdles and O. P. Ingles as Justice. Said Ingles is an old acquaintance of mine formerly in the shoe business in Buffalo. About half past nine the Judges arrived and one Notary Public to swear them in. Two McArdles and a McQuin were the Judges. One of them could not write his name had to make his mark in signing his affidavit. The Notary Public and the old man McArdle were appointed clerks of Election. One of this number had to have a deputy to write for him, and still he had to keep the poll list. The Ballot Box was an old sugar box imported from Omaha for the occasion. It was tied together with a string and a hole cut in the top with a table knife while the judges were at breakfast. There was some 500 votes sent out and most of them different still it took about an hour to get the votes ready to suit the twenty voters. At last the voters were sent out doors and the breakfast table dishes and all was shoved up to the door and the polls declared open, and I had the great honor of casting the first vote that was ever cast in the pappillion district. I am the first man that ever voted in this presinct. I had many chances to immortalize my name all of which I respectfully declined.

Having deposited our votes as every honest man who has the good of his country at heart should do Darling and myself started back to our claim taking with us a man whom I engaged to break up 20 acres of prarie to have it ready to put in my crops next spring. Returning I finished the course of the Pappio as it crosses my farm and sit down to close up my writing on the claim.

Last evening when we went to the Germans to get our bread and milk we noticed they had company who had come three miles from the north west. One woman and a little girl about twelve years old I thought I had seen before and inquired where they were from and learned they were from the east some where and were of german decent. Made no further inquiries after they left. I learned the woman and little girl had been enquiring who I was and where I was from. They of cours got no more information than I did. This morning The little girl came to the Election with Mr Ingles who proved to be her father. Mr Ingles said his wife told him she saw a man down on the prarie she had seen somewhere before. The mystery was now solved. They used to live in Buffalo and the little girl took the Casket and she and her mother used to come to the office for it. The little girls dress did not compair with other children on the prarie she looked like a rose among thistles. It seemes go where you will even on the wild praries of Nebraska you will find some one you have seen before.

It is now past one o'clock P. M. and I will put up my writing and stow away things ready to start for Omaha about ten tonight so as not to get in untill after midnight as I have to swear I have lived on my claim five days and nights and slept regularly there as well as cooked and eat and at this time it is my residence.

Instead of waiting until ten we left at four P. M. and passed around to the west to look at some other claims and arrived in Omaha between eight and nine at night. Much to my surprise I only found two letters and both those were unimport one from Mr De Puy and Mr Hall. Did not sleep well this night.

*Tuesday 4.* — Got up early. Waited at the land office untill 8 o'clock A. M. found my turn would come until tomorrow. Filed on the land and got an attourney to make out my papers. Rode up to Saratoga with Mr Tuttle and got my washing and put on a white shirt again. Walked to Omaha. Got the "Home" and "Casket" for August and two important letters one from Mr. Gridley in relation to Mr Turners buying the Niagara St property. The result of his confab with the Turners was not very satisfactory. Mr. G. will see them and write again soon. The Second letter was from E. S. Rich to whom I sold the notes I had from Wowzer. He says all has now been paid excep one hundred a fifty dollars for that he holds Mr. Wowzers note endorsed by Mr. Steele. He Mr Rich thinks that we shall neither of us loose anything although all the parties who made the note I sold him have failed even to Miller, Orton and Mulligan.

Mr Gridley writes discouraging of prospects in Buffalo. He says failures are of frequent occurrance, that prospects are much better in

Omaha than in Buffalo. This fact I was before aware of particular to those who had capital to do with or to those in business. I have neither business or capital and I have about come to the conclusion that this is not the place for me this fall and winter. More of this at another time.

After tea went up to Mr Tuttles and had a long conversation with him. I am determined to bring certain matters to a focus and that at once. I make an occasional strike here but I cannot stand it to be so idle as I have been here. This fall and winter is a better time here for people with money.

*Wednesday 5.* — *Ten o'clock A. M*  I have proved up and got my papers am now an owner of real estate in Nebraska Territory am the proprietor of Rock Brook Farm. Will now introduce a map of said farm made while on the premices and give a description of the same:—

### Rock Brook Farm

*The Name* — The name suggested itself when we first visited the place, a few weeks since. The scarcity of stone in the streams in this territory is so universal, that a stream filled, as in the eastern and middle states, with rock, attracts no little attention and becomes quite an object of curiosity. There are many Indian names familiar to the place, that might sound more poetical and pleasing to the ears of Eastern peaple, who have spent their days among the hills and rocks which characterize their peculiar locality. Such names however are not as attractive to us of the western praries, who are amidst the Indians and their relics, as the name which expresses that which is most *rare* in our midst, and calls to our retentive memories the seenes of our childhood which were spent by the "babling brook."

Rock Brook Farm, is a name peculiarly adapted to the place as it has a brook almost the entire length of which is filled with gravel and common rock, and brook stone, the like of which I think cannot be found within hundreds of miles of this farm.

The amount pre-empted is only 160 acres and is comprised within the red and black lines on the Map. The 80 acres on the west and enclosed with black only is held only by claim but being pre-empted as it is on all sides I trust I shall find no difficulty in holding it until the land comes in market, as few persons can be found that are willing to loose their right of pre-emption for 80 acres unless it is very valuable. I have pre-empted all that portion which has timber and Rock, and the part I *think* has coal on, the balance is naked prarie.

*The Pappillon* — This stream which runs through the East end of the farm, heads many miles to the north-west and drains an extensive reagion of country. The valley or bottoms of this stream is from one to three miles wide and the richest portion of this Territory. The Papillon's and Platt valleys are now considered the most valuable, and will very soon surpass the Mohawk valley and the valleys of the Wyoming. They are now mostly valuable for the grass they yield, which makes the best hay in the county. About 60 or 80 acres of Rock Brook Farm is bottom land. Of the Pappillon's there is three the first or Little, 2d The Big, and 3d the west Pappillon. Ours is on the Big Pappillon a stream at this time fifteen to twenty feet across and four feet deep, this is its dryest time. During heavy rain storms in the upper country it has been known to rise 17 feet in three hours. The banks to that depth are very steep. In the the bottoms sometimes overflow.

The name Pappillon is French and Indian means butterfly. It is called mostly Pappio and will probably be known only in english as Pappio.

*The Nin na bah* Is very noted among the Indians. It is an Indian name signifying singing water, or babling watter. From time immemorial the indians have camped on this stream. It makes about half mile above my southwest corner is composed of springs. In an ordinary time there is sufficient watter to carry one run of mill stones. There is a good mill site on it I think. It drains many thousand acres and in a rain storm gets up to ten feet in depth and as much in width. The stone and rock seemed to have been depostid by some volcanic action. The stone is at least half Iron when broken resembles cast Iron more than it does stone.

*Black Walnut Grove* — This grove is in a gorge formed by a ravine coming down a bluff from the south. It is filled and bounded on the east with huge sand stone rock and bolders. This grove was the favorite camping ground of the Omahas but not large enough for one fourth of a tribe to camp in. Every fall and spring the prarie fires make sad havoc among the timber which otherwise would increase rapidly. As it is there is sufficient for one family with carefull usage until more is grown. Timber fringes the Ninnabah for about a half mile but except this grove it is cottonwood and elm.

*Turkey foot Rock*    This is the largest rock in the grove and forms the base of a high bluff and the west boundry of the Ninnabah. It is of immence size being some 40 feet along the stream and twenty foot high. How far it runs into the bluff it is impossible to ascertain. Back of these rocks in the bluffs we believe there is coal if any where in this region. The rock is very soft composed of sand which is easily cut with any sharp instrument. Could be removed as rapidly as any clay bank. Is to soft for building purposes. It is carved with many devices by the Indians one of which resembles a Turkeys foot hence we give it the name of Turkey foot Rock.

*Pipe Clay Rock* — This rock is the same as the other on the south bank of the stream but not as large. At the base along the ninnabah is a peculiar kind of white clay from which the Indians mould pipes and dry them in the sun useing them without baking. In cutting off chunks from these Rocks, near the base one finds balls of clay as large as a cocoe nut in the midst of the rock. This is considered best by the Indians. I think the clay valuable. For want of a better name we call this Pipe Clay Rock.

*Skelleton Rock* — This rock is of the same formation as the others but smaller. The principal feature is the origin of the name we have given it. The spring following Aug 1. 1854 Darling went out to make further observations on his claim and visit parts he had not before seen. Crossing the Ninnabah in the bend and going upon the bluff that covered this rock he discovered a human skelliton streatched out at full length its arm across its chest. Every particle of flesh and clothing had disappeared and the bones were bleached white. The sight so shocked Darling that he instinctively grasped his rifle and placed his finger upon the trigger and looked around to see if any one was in sight. He says had he seen a human being he is not sure but his first act would have been to fire upon him so strong and strange was his fear at the sight of the skelliton. After a little he went up to, and examined the skelliton. Through the skull a bullet had passed, showing how he come to his death. It was the frame of a powerfull man. In removing the skull, the joints were so fastened by a glutenous substance, that he turned the body near half over before the bones seperated at the joints of the skull and neck. As soon as the skull was removed Darling passed his larette through the throat and eye hung it upon the pommel of his saddle and galloped into town. This incident has caused the name of *skelliton Rock* to be attached as it is.

*Darlings Spring* — This is named in memory of Dick Darling. He had always been so attached to this spring he could not refrain from Ditching it as he had previously planed even after it was sold. This he done while with me proving up and a hard job it was too.

*Omaha Buffalo Trail* — The peculiarities of this curiosity is described in my diary under date of Aug. 1st.

Having completed my description, I will take a walk and let it close the business of the day continuing as usual my diary.

*Thursday, 6* Immedidely after breakfast went up to Mr Tuttles who had agreed to go out to my farm with me. We harnessed up and in company with his brother-in-law started, going by Saratoga we stoped and selected a location for the warehouse.

Reaching the claim house we found some one had broke in and stole two Buffalo Robes and our beef. We attributed it to the Pawne Indians. We wandered over most of the farm. Mr Tuttle and Zoller were both very much pleased with it. Seem to think as much of it as I do. We did not reach Omaha on our return until four in the afternoon. Brought back all my effects from the cabin and sold the cabin on the ground for twelve dollars to one of the McArdles who wishes also to preempt.

About bed time I learned there was to be a danse on the Steamer "Ben Bolt" which had come down this day from Sioux City. Hoping to see Miss Clark I went down but they were so long in getting to dancing I did not stop. Only had a glimse of Miss C.

*Friday, 7* — Was awoke this morning by Jake coming into my room and handing me a letter Mr Cook gave him. It proved to be a bill of lading of my things which had come during the night on the Steamer Omaha. Hurried on my clothes and went down to the levee where I found all safe and sound to all appearances except through a crack I could see some pieces of looking-lass. The steamer had gone up to Sioux City but left the bill for collection the whole amount of which was $64.45 a little cheaper than I had expected. The charges from St Louis here was only $1. per hundred while from Chicoga to St Louis it was $1.21 1/2 double what it ought to have been. Altogether however I am satisfied. I must now find a place to store them as it is uncertain when and where I shall want to use them. After breakfast went up to Saratoga and devoted the balance of the day to some improvements there.

*Saturday. 8* Busied myself at Saratoga this forenoon. Afternoon settled my freight bill and done some figuring. Getting very uneasy and am bringing every thing on the square and am only awaiting a letter from Br Frank which I shall probably receive within a week, when I shall make some decided move. We have to day the Stamers "Hannabal" and "Minnehaha" in from St. Louis.

*Sunday, 9* — Another month has passed making five since I left home. Long as the time has seemed from week to week I cannot realize I have been five months away. Why within that time there must be a preceptible difference or change in the growth of my children and if I should be still other five months before I see them I suppose they will outgrow my recollection. It is not probable however that I shall be much longer from them at this time. If however it was deemed for the best I could remain from my family this fall and winter, but as matters have turned out here my stay in Omaha is very short for this time.

This has been one of the hotest days of the Season and all we have been able to do is to keep cool. This afternoon went up to Mr. Zollers where Mr. Tuttle boards spent a pleasant two hours and to dinner with them.

*Monday 10* Last night there came up a rain storm accompanied with a hurricain which blew down a building I was interested in in Saratoga. The frame was only up and the damage will be easily repired. During the storm some of our neighbors who were living in temporary shanties became frightened, and for better safety came over to the generals and stoped until the fury of the storm had passed.

The Steamer (I can't think its name) came in this morning and brought Cooks House-hold goods. He not feeling very well I received them for him. Went up to Tuttles rode up to Saratoga with him. I stopped until the building (which by the way was intended for my private residence, which I have not before spoken of,) was raised again. Walked down to Omaha and got two letters one from wife and one from R. Adams. Answered wifes and maled all of Diary to Aug. 10th 2 o'clock P. M. E. F BEADLE

*Tuesday, 11* After what I had written yesterday was mailed, I procured some nails and repaired the damages on my boxes of house hold goods and had them placed in the warehouse to be stored until further orders. In the evening helped Cook unpack his things. Found in one of the boxes the cain I brought to this place and on my return left by mistake at Cooks in Flint Mich. The steamer Edenburgh came in just at night.

This day I have devoted in part to writing letters to parties east and closing up my affairs here, this afternoon started with Mr Tuttle and his team to go over to the Bluffs. The wind so bothered the ferry that we abandoned the trip for to-day. We have a hot south wind blowing strongly.

*Wednesday 12* — Went over to the Bluffs with Mr Tuttle spent the day without incident of interest, visiting the printing offices.

This night is the opening dance at the Central House Saratoga. Should like to be there but cannot as it comes my turn to take care of Dick Darling tonight. He is here at the Generals sick with the billious fever. Came in from claim hunting last Saturday quite sick. On Sunday we got him down here. He is doing as well as can be expected. Has the best of care.

*Thursday 13.* After breakfast walked up to Saratoga to close up my affairs there. Never saw Saratoga look so inticeing particularly the point where I have been building and sold out last week. Counted 56 buildings completed, and others in course of erection. There are many towns east that claim importance that have no more buildings than Saratoga at this time. From the Central House I rode down in the Omnabus, by the bluff route or the route where the best buildings are along the edge of the bluff. I could hardly realize the change that had taken place directly under my own eyes. When I came here in the spring there was but two houses on the site. Now there was almost a city graded streets veheacles of all kinds and two lines of Omnibuses. The omnibus ride reminded me of the ride from Cold Springs to Buffalo except the beauty if the scenery which Buffalo cannot compare with.

This afternoon has been very hot. Cook and myself have been on the look-out for a boat as Lib is expected every boat. About the middle of the afternoon a severe thunder storm come up which has lasted untile evening. About this time a boat made its appearance at the lower landing on the bluff side some six miles below here. It would not of course be up here until morning. Cook will probably watch it all night.

Made arangements to retire early to make up for the lack of sleep last night. Got my coat off when Cook came down to get some milk. Said "they had come." Meaning his wife and children. I waited for the milk and took it up. Found them all as natural as could be excep Lib was very thin and poor. Ella knew me and such a hugging and kissing as she gave me. I have not head since I left Sophia. I think Hatta recollects me but we did not get acquainted so as to talk much. I gave some milk undressed her and got her to sleep. Lib was tired out she was so anxious to get here after she started. She changed conveyance as often as I was obliged to when I cam. At Belleview twelve miles below by land but near thirty by the river she learned the boat would not reach Omaha that night and she could not think of being another night on the boat. So a conveyance was found by one of the passengers a Mr. Barkalow, a brother deacon in the same church with Mr Cook, and they rode up by land taking Cook very much by surprise when he was at supper at his boarding house. Cook having his house all in readiness they drove there at once. Bought some bread. I took up milk and commenced house keeping the first meal. At about ten I returned to the Generals and went to bed.

Four brick columns of the Capitol and the brick work which rested on them fell just at night. The cause I have not yet learned. Presume however the weight was to great for the columns. It will cost a Number of thousand dollars to repair the damage.

*Friday, 14*   Dark cloudy and lowry day. Helped Cook put up shelving and regulate. I seemes still more like home to see lib and the children here.

Received letters from Mr. Myers Irwin and my sister Sarah. In Sarah's letter which was written the 5th in which she says "Frank wrote me last Wednesday that Mate would start for O in ten days." Hear again I heare in a round-about way something which I should have understood fully if the letter Frank wrote me had not been miscarried. I was in hopes it would turn up yet. It is now so late it probably never will and tomorrow or Monday I shall probably receive another as it will then be tiem to get an answer from one I wrote complaining of delay which has annoyed me for near a month.

*Saturday 15* — Weather same as yesterday. No mail from the East. Steamers "Watassa" "Hesperian" and "Alonzo Child" in this evening. The Alonzo Child was not expected until tomorrow (Sunday) night in that case she would not have left until Monday noon when Mr Tuttle and a number of others would would be ready to go, together with myself provided the letter I am expecting should arrive. As it is she will go down in the morning and we must await the next chance. The Alonzo Child is a superior boat and Makes good time.

About dark a thunder storm came up and it rained in torrents and when we went to bed the storm seemed at its height. But what is most unusual here during a thunder storm there is no wind the thunder and lightning makes up for that. The storm is becoming to terriffic for me to write and I will turn in and see if I can sleep.

*Sunday Morning Aug 16, 1857*   Such a terriffic night as has just passed I never in my life have experienced. An hour after going to bed the storm seemed to double its violence. The rain did not seem to come in drops but come down in a body so that the ground looked like a lake. Roof siding and brick walls seemed to be of little use as the rain came in until it was near an inch in depth on the floor. The lightning was one continual blaze and the thunder come clapp after clapp seeming to roll across the roof of the house while it shook and trembled in every timber. Every instant I feared the house would tumble as I beleived the lightning was strikeing in every direction around us and the next we all feared would strike the house. The storm continued thus for about an hour when it subsided to a respectable thunder storm such as we have east. The sesation was only to get a fresh start when it come on again and so it continued during the whole of last night and did not cease raining until after daylight. I cannot conceive where all the watter could have been got that fell last night. The first effect of the lightning discovered this morning was on the Capitol. One of the columns and the work it supported had been struck and leveled with earth. There is undoubtedly other serious injuries that we shall see when we go out around. We all thought our chances slim last night, but have come out right. Afternoon find no further damage from lightning. Walls of buildings have fallen and settled and cellars filled with water causing great destruction of property.

*Monday 17*   No letters today except one from Cousin Jennie in Indiana. Have decided to wait no longer for the letter than until the first boat when I shall go letter or no letter. I can travail almost as cheap as I can remain here and I have now no business but to wait. Walked up to Saratoga this after noon. Another column of the Capitol fell today. Weather cool and pleasant.

*Tuesday 18*   Still no letter or boat and it is the hardest kind of work to wait when one is all ready to go. Yesterday and today people have been very busy in putting up lightning rods. I think there has been a hundred put up since the last storm.

*Wednesday 19.*   Letters from wife and Frank today all satisfactory. Rode up to Saratoga and back with Mr. Tuttle in the forenoon. Afternoon wrote letters. No boat yet in sight. We are at this time longer without a boat than we have been since the boats commenced running this season. The time seems long and moves slow. One year ago this night I left Buffalo the first time to come to Omaha.

*Thursday 20* — Still no boat up today. The "Dan Converse" running between this point and Sioux City is down to-day and may go on to

St. Louis in the moning. She is a small cockkle-shell of a stern wheeler. I shall however be tempted to take passage on her. The fare will be no more and if the time is longer shall get more corn and bacon and bed-bugs and no extra charges.

*Friday 21.* — Nine o'clock this morning rode up with Mr Griffin three miles to his farm. Had a good supply of mellons. Received directions to purchase and forward seeds and trees. After dinner walked back to Omaha. Found no boats up. The "Dan Converse" however was just ready to leave would wait half hour. Hurried up to F. Gridley & Co's Bank and got a money package I was to take east. Dodged into Cooks, to say I was off and away I went Tuttle taking my things to the boat. In an hour after my mind was made up I was on board bag and baggage and at quarter after four we shoved off into the "big Muddy" once more to try the uncertanty of this treacherous river. It was with feelings of deep regret that I saw the city fade in the distance. I have seldom been in a place I have formed such an attachment for as Omaha. The evening was delightful and we sped down with the current rapidly laying up for the night at a wood yard a mile below Plattsmouth on the Iowa side. Our supper was hard and did not tell well for the first meal.

*Saturday 22* — At daylight got under way and returned to Plattsmouth for passengers remained two hours went three miles and run upon a sand-bar where we remained until after 4 o'clock P. M. when the Packet "Watossa" running between St. Joseph and Omaha came along and was hailed to takon three of our number who were disposed to abandon the "Dan Converse." We had all of us worked more or less to help get off the boat but seemingly to no effect. The captain of the Watossa came on board and from him we learned what we had previously began to fear that the chances were against our getting of at all as the boat had run into the wrong channel or what seamed to be the channel and passed over barrs which rubed hard with the current to assist. The water had fallen and to get back seemed impossible. Add to this the Converse had her last stick of wood under the boilers and her miserable fare had almost starved us. As fast as the Watossa's small boat could carry them the passengers left the "Dan Converse" to the number of over

forty leaving but about fifteen on board who I think will be obliged
to abandon at last. The boat was poorly manned and only wanted to
get to St. Louis to be delivered to her creditors. Some of the passengers
on the Dan Convers had paid only to St Josephs, ten dollars, while
others myself among the number had paid to St. Louis, Twenty dollars.
Not one dime would the Captain refund. All plead and expostulated
with him but to no effect. It was thought best however to leave and
loose what we had paid. I was personally acquainted with the clerk and
when he saw me leaving he called me into the office and on his own
responsibility paid me back ten dollars with the injunctions of secrecy
from the other passengers.

All that were disposed being aboard the Wotossa we left a cord of
wood for the "Dan convers" and went on our way like a racer.

The contrast from the Dan Convers to the Watossa was like changing
from life on the plains to the Astor or St. Nicholas N. Y. Although
smaller than the Dan Convers the Watossa was a perfect palace, and the
supper we got, which was ready as we went aboard, had an injurious
effect on some of the passengers who pertook too freely trying to make
up for their fasting on the Da*m* Converse.

The Watosa only running to St Joseph we could only pay to that point
the price was the same as from Omaha, ten dollars making double fare.
We made a fine run the balance of the day. At night we were many of us
obliged to take a matrass on the floor but they were clean and without
bugs while on the Dan Converse we found *bed bugs on the table cloth* at
supper even.

*Sunday 23* — Got an early start. Had a delightfull day. Being cloudy
we could occupy the Hurricane deck and the ever changing views were
charming. We laid up within thirty miles of st Joseph. This evening
was introduced to Mrs. Bloomer of the Bloomer Costume who resides
at Council Bluffs. Is on her way to Seneca falls N. Y. on a visit. Had
an interesting conversation of an hour when I took my mattress and
straighend out on the Cabin floor.

*Monday 24* The fog this morning prevented our getting under way
until eight o'clock so that we did not reach St Josephs until eleven

o'clock two hours too late for the packet. Three boats had left this morning had the fog not detained us we would have been in time to have made a good bargain as the three boats were in opposition.

The Captain of the Watossa who is a perfect gentleman, at a very little solicitation, took us to Weston sixty miles further where we found the Cataract of the Lightning line. This line runs boats daily between Weston and Jefferson City and connects with the R. R. to St Louis fare through $13. Some twenty of our number took passage on the Cataract when the Watossa decided to go ten miles further to Leavenworth City the balance continued on to Leavenworth. The Cataract is a mail boat and must leave Weston on time which is tomorrow afternoon half past three. We were Late on the Cataract but they got us up a supper after which I took a stroll up town. This is the place where the little girl was burried this spring on my upward trip. Retired to bead early.

*Tuesday 25* Beleive this is wife's birthday. After Breakfast took my cane and note book to reconnoitre. Between Weston an Leavenworth City distance by land seven and half miles. Crossed the ferry at Weston into Kansas and had a Most delightful walk to Leavenworth City through a delightful region of country. Stopped at Fort Leavenworth on the route. The soldiers were on parade. It was a fine sight. Reached Leavenworth City about eleven A. M. rested a short time and then examined the town. It is in my opinion *one* of the best points on the river and must be a great city unless their high prices kill it.

Here I learn the Watossa overtook one of the boats from from St. Joseph. The "D. A. January" who took the Watassas passengers but did not leave until about nine o'clock this morning so we shall be in St Louis probably a day a head of it as *It* runs through and we cut off 174 miles by R. R. It is now about half past three and it is probable the Catteract will be along soon. I have spent the last hour writing up my Diary, and to Cook in the office of the "Kansas Herald."

At 5 o'clock the Cataract came along and I was again rushing down the Big Muddy at more than ordinary speed. We made Kansas City and laid up for the night.

*Wednesday 26* — A fine day. We made good time, 190 miles. Intended to reach Glasgow ten miles farther but at dark we run on a sand bar and was late before we got off. Had a thunder shower this evening.

*Thursday 27* — Another fine day. Made Jifferson City in time for the train with half hour to spare. The cars left at two o'clock P. M. with a full load of passengers mostly like myself eager to join their families. If I ever enjoyed or fully realized a seat in the cars it was on this occassion. The sensation was very much like that felt in coming in sight of the old home one has not seene for years. But as he now beholds it in the distance he almost fancies he sees the smiling faces and grasps the friendly hands he has so long been seperated from. Yes the sensation experienced on taking a seat and getting under motion once more on the Cars was like being within sight of home and friends. True it is a thousand miles yet, but what is a thousand miles of railroad, distance is annihilated and we cannot realize it. I feele I am now almost home. Nine o'clock at night found me comfortable located in that best of homes for the traveler *The Barnum House*. Its superior cannot be found in the country.

As soon as we got into St Louis I could notice the difference in the air we breathed. To me directly from the praries of nebraska where the air is pure and wholesom, it seemed almost stifling and as the omnibus went around from house to house, delivering passengers, through filthy streets and lanes, I was forsed to hold my handkerchief to my nose, to prevent the stench from sickening me. Undoubtedly I should not have noticed it had I come directly from Buffalo. But I had now got weaned from the delicious odor of a city.

*Friday 28* — The money I brought for Mr Gridley all had to be exchanged at this place which kept me busy until the cars were about to leave. I was in time however to take the morning tran at eleven o'clock, and reached Sandoval quarter before two P. M. Checked my baggage down to Centralia and there being no cars for a number of hours I walked down and reached Hatts at a little before four. Found them all well and pleased as well as surprised to see me. The first question was where is Mate and the children supposing I was from the East and they with me. Before going to Harriets I stoped at the post office and got a letter from Mate under date of the 20th. Harriet and Charlotte have much to say about my rusty appearance. They say I look so black and forlorn they are ashamed of me. I have not worn a cravat for two or three months. I will try and get civilized by the time I reach Cooperstown.

*Saturday 29* — Received a letter from Br. Frank. Devoted the forenoon to writing. Afternoon tended baby while Harriet done me some washing. Bailey and Tom went out last night on the train to return tonight again.

*Sunday, 30* — Visited with Bailey and Thomas. Have decided to leave here tonight half past nine so as to get into Chicago in the forenoon and leave the same Evening. Should I wait until tomorrow and go up on the train with Bailey and Thomas it would bring me into Chicago at midnight.

Had a supper of boiled prarie chickens which was the greatest luxury I have had this season. The conductor on the train I was to go out on called here this evening. Said he would fix me through to Chicago.

*Chicago Monday 31* — Arrived here on time ten minutes before nine A. M. had a pleasant night slept some. Found Mr. Lyman who was pleased to see me. Took dinner and supper with him. Here I learn that the Reciprocity Bank of Buffalo closed its doors last Saturday. Every dollar I have is on that bank. It is not much but sufficient to pay my fair to Buffalo. I must try my chances. A report is in circulation here respecting Mr. Brayman which astonishes me. Mr Lyman thinks I am looking like a pioneer.

*Lake Erie on board Steamer Mississippi Tuesday Sept 1, 57* Again I am rejoiced at being on the clear waters of this beautiful Lake. The contrast from the muddy watters of the Missourie is delightful. I think at this time and for the sake of a little variety I would like to have a littl e bit of a gale on the lake. There is however no prospects as the air is still and the sky clear.

Last evening the cars left at 8 o'clock. When The conductor came along I gave him my check for my baggage and told him how I was situated and I would fix it in Detroit. Which I did do on seeing Mr Frazer. On reaching Marshal this morning before daylight we were two hours behind time. Two miles after leaving marshal one of the driving wheels of the Locomotive came off and we were obliged to send back to Marshal for a Locomotive to come and draw us into Marshal then go out again and bring in the crippled engine. This detained us four hours so we did not reach Detroit until one o'clock P. M. when we were due seven o'clock A. M. We were however fortunate in having the Captain of the Steamer on the cars so the boat did not leave until our arrival. At 2 o'clock P. M. we were driving down the clear waters of Detroit river and by the time dinner was over we were out into the lake ploughing toward Buffalo.

I learn today on the boat that the Hollister Bank and White's Bank both of Buffalo have failed. Can't tell how true it is. I say blessed be nothing.

We have had a delightfull evening which has been enjoyed by large number of passengers who remained out on deck enjoying moonlight on the water. At nine o'clock dancing was commenced and I retired.

*Wednesday — 2d*  Got up after a good nights sleep at six o'clock. Found we were still some thirty miles out. A slight fog and the smoke of the city so enveloped it we could not get a vew of the town until we rounded the light house. I remained on the boat until all the passengers had left watching for my cane which had been stolen on the boat. Was not successfull in finding it. Took my satchel in hand and walked slowly up the familliar streets to Irwins store. Found all seemingly pleased to see me. Breakfasted and read letters returned from Omaha and one from Br. Frank and wife received this morning. Answered letters and made a few calls during the forenoon. Afternoon made some business calls, among which was one on the Turner Brothers. Passed by our house on Niagara Street. Did it not look familiar? The door stood open and I was almost tempted to go in. I looked in vain for wife and children, they came not to greet me. My friends seeme all rejoiced to see me and overwhelm me with questions. All have their remarks to make. One says "you look like a returned Calafornian" another "you are a regular border ruffian in earnest." All agree in saying I look thin. I am afflicted with boils sufficient to make any one look thin.

The city looks close and cluttered to me. I presume that is owing to my having been where they give more scope to the streets and lay out cities on a more Magnificient scale and dont build their houses so high or close together. I did not think I looked quite so much like a ruffian until I got here to Buffalo where I find every one with their best clothes on and their faces and hands look as though they had been out to bleach.

Lib and Sister Sarah took pity on me soon after I arrived, one mended up my coat while the others took some oil and a comb and tried to limber up and put my hair in shape. Irwin let me wear one of his cast off hats, and thus attired I looked about half civilized. I think by the time I get to Cooperstown I shall begin to look natural and become civilized so that my family may not disown me.

Spent this evening standing in the door of Irwins store watching the people as they pass. More particularly the Ladies. They look very interesting. I had almost become so accostomed to being a widower that I saw little or nothing to attract my attention between the sexes. I now however, where there are so many facinating creatures pasing every moment, am not quite as insensible to the difference and feele quite an in-clination in favor of the ladies.

Irwin has been so full of his jokes and fun aided by Robert that I am myself again and feele like quite a different man. Have been so longe alone, no wife children or relation to speak with I had become so Morose and mopish I was not my natural self. I think I will now fat up if I can get rid of my Boils. I find Irwin looking better than I have ever seen him. His business is good, and he is cherfull, and now knows how to manage the business with ease.

*Thursday 3* — Did not sleep well last night owing to the pain of a boil which bid fair to be a severe one. After breakfast went over to Dr. Grays. Had him drive a lance into it less than an inch and then burn it with an acostic. It felt fine for a short time hope it will kill it with the aid of poltices.

Spent the forenoon in business connected with the house and lot. Afternoon went out to Cold Springs by way of Niagara, Virginia, Ninth and Cottage streets in company with Robert. Met Mrs. Hodge and Mrs House on Delaware St. near the church going a visiting. They were rejoiced to see me passed on to the house wher Joseph met me on the sidewalk and made such a nois Sarah come out to see what was the matter. Had a pleasant hour and as many pears as I could eat. Find their new house up the first story. Great changes are going on. Mr Wackermons house is up as well as Mr Huns the latter is finished. It made me feele lonesome to see the improvements all of which are attributed, and I think justly, to my moveing into the neighborhood. They have commenced paving Main st to Cold Spring. The tax on the lot my house was on will be about $400. It will be a good investment.

Called on Mrs Halbert. Found there a widow of one of Mr. Halberts Brothers or cousins her maiden name was Estabrook a cousin of Gen. Estabrook of Omaha. She was pleased to meet me so recently from where her cousin resided. Returned to Irwin's in time for a supper of broild chicken.

*Friday–4* — Found qute a number ready to negotiate for the house and lot on Niagara street. Ther terms do not however suit me. Received a letter from the Turner Brothers which was returned to me from Omaha. Said letter contains a proposition which I shall accept if I can do no better. Suffered severely from my boil all day. Received a letter from Frank.

*Saturday–5* — Figured considerable about the house and lot but as yet have come to no terms with any one. I have a week left still to operate in. A few will get disappointed I can assure them.

*Sunday 6* — Quite cool this morning. Spent the forenoon in writing. Afternoon took a stroll with Irwin up Niagara st and across to Mr. Vanduze's where we took tea, per invitation from Mr and Mrs V. extended to me in person this morning by Mr. V. We had a very pleasant walk and chat about old times, present times and the future. Got home just at dusk when Irwin and his wife, Miss Myers and Myself took a walk down to the steamboat landing. This is the first time I have walked out with the Ladies in Six Months.

I find Buffalo desecrates the Sabath as much as any western town I ever heard of. This noon a fire company come from N. Y. on the Cars.

When they were met by one of this city companies and paraded the streets with a band of music, and drawing their Engine. This shocked me, in New orleans it might do. If the papers are not down on it I am mistaken.

*Monday 7* — Have had a busy day in negotiating with parties about the House and lot. Took Mr Hotchkiss up to look at it. It did not look like my home or as my home does when my wife presides. Found the grape vine as full as it Could hold. It is a sight worth looking at. Called this afternoon at Mrs. Brown's to see Mrs. Meachem. She was on a visit to Albany. Feele rather lonesome this evening but not as much so as I did at times in Omaha. Am still visiting with Irwin. Will be a boarder as soon as I get employment.

*Tuesday 8* — Figured up my expencs for traveling the last year and find I must hold up as all is now gone and I have no hopes. Believe it my best plan to take the $15. it would cost me to go to Cooperstown and use it to get to living again. Nothing new today.

*Wednesday 9* — Still figuring about the house and lot but as yet no sale. Got the blues some.

*Thursday 10* — Letters from Frank and Mate. Thought I had the bues yesterday but give it up. Did not know what the blues was.

*Friday 11.* — Sold ten Dollars Reciprocity Money for five dollars currant. My 36th berthday and the most unpleasant one I ever recollect to have passed.

*Saturday 12* — New costomers for the house and lot. No sale however as yet.

*Sunday 13.* Received letter from Brother Frank. Heard some unpleasant news.

*Monday 14*  This day visited the orphan Assylum and County poor house. At quarter past eleven at night took the cars en route to Coperstown.

*Tuesday 15* — Reached Fortplain at 8 o'clock A. M. Started immediately on foot towards Cooperstown. Six miles from Fort Plain met Wife and Irwin coming in a buggy after me. Arrived at Cooperstown two o'clock P. M.

*16, 17, 18, & 19*  Spent in visiting and figuring up some business for the winter.

*Sunday 20* — Walked up to the old homestead in company with Br. Frank some of the way rainy. Irwins 10th birth day the first spent in this place where he was born.

*Monday 21* — Figured with Mr. Bolls about engaging for the winter in selling patent rights for Camera Box. A supposed improvement for the Deguereon operator.

*Tuesday 22* — Started at Seven o'clock A. M. with Br. Frank for Franklin to visit our Mother and Sister. Stoped at a hop yard on the East side of the Susquehanna one or two miles below Milford Village and took in Cornelia Armstrong. Arrived in Franklin village about two o'clock P. M. Found our mother quite low but recovering from an attack of dysentery which had come near proving fatal. Concidering all things we had a pleasant visit.

*Wednesday 23* — Left Franklin village on our return about 10 o'clock A. M. Dined at Oneonta with friend Pick. Left Cornelia where we found her and reached Cooperstown Six in the evening.

*Thursday 24* — Experimented in taking views with the Patent camera box preparatory to going out selling patents.

*Friday and Saturday 25 & 26* — Not important.

*Sunday, 27* — Rode up to Father Penningtons and took dinner. Took up Mate and Sophia. Irwin remained at home on account of a boil on his face. Evening walked out with Frank and Cockett.

*Monday 28* — Wife and children left in the noon stage for Alden N. Y. en route to Buffalo. Afternoon very lonesome.

*Tuesday, 29* —Experimented with the Patent Camera Box.

*Wednesday, 30* — Otsego County Agricultural Fair. Assisted Brother Frank in his store. Had a very busy day of it and a good trade. Received $1.50 for my services, being sufficient to pay stage fare to Railroad.

*Thursday, Oct. 1* — First frost of the season at this place, ice formed in the washbasin out of doors. Walked out of town at seven o'clock. Was soon overtaken by the stage. Was the only passenger the first ten miles. The sun rose clear and soon dispelled the fog that hung over the Lake. The ride along the west side of the lake was delightfull. Still it reminded me strongly of the time I left Cooperstown ten years previous in the Month of December, with a view — if the place suited me — of taking up my residence in Buffalo. At that time I was the only passenger the entire route to Fort Plain. It was in the midst of a thaw and no snow on the ground. The roads were in such condition it was not deemed safe to use the Coach, and a lumber waggon was substituted. In the center of this waggon I took my seat the lone passenger, some of the way moving at a snail pace at others going at a breakneck speed. All day through a drizzling rain. At Cooperstown I was leaving Father, Mother, Brothers, sisters wife and baby, the baby not three months old. But young as it was, it was one of the motive powers that indused me to try a new home. And it was with a sad heart that I crossed the susquehanna on that morning (the road on the east side of the lake was not then completed) not knowing when if ever I should recross it to visit my friends and native place. The convenianc of travel as well as the expence has greatly changed for the benefit of the traveler since that time, and I cannot recollect the number of times I have since visited Cooperstown at all seasons of the year and under varied circumstances sometimes on business of a commercial nature, sometimes to meet with my Brothers and Sisters to gladden the hearts of our parents, sometimes with my family and at one time to follow my Fathers remains to the grave.

The past ten years has been full of changes with me and I feel very much as I did ten years ago when I left Cooperstown not knowing if I should ever be called on business or by my own inclination again to return. My friends and relatives have become scattered and I am myself out of business and unsettled and may take up my residence in the far west. In all the visits I have made to C. during the last ten years, I have never left the place as I did at that time until this day. The *only passenger in the Coach*. This fact has tended to make me feele sad and gloomy and to ruminate on the past. At about 8 o'clock I bid adieu to Lake Otsego and sooner than I expected we wheeled up to the Hotel at Hallsville. There we took in more passengers and my train of thought was changed.

*End of the Diary*

# Index